Teaching Life

Life Lessons for Aspiring (and Inspiring) Teachers

Todd Shy

AVENUES THE WORLD SCHOOL PRESS

AVENUES THE WORLD SCHOOL PRESS

11 Madison Square North
17th Floor
New York, NY
10010-1420 USA
https://press.avenues.org

ISBN: 979-8-9850518-0-3

For William, Emily, and Katie

CONTENTS

INTRODUCTION

So many books about schools involve big policy proposals, broad culture complaints, and jeremiads about America's declining position in the world of learning. They are long on critique and advice, short on inspiration. When teachers themselves are addressed in books, it's usually in the form of nuts and bolts—how to write curriculum, how to manage a classroom—as if the vision and inspiration for teaching young people just happens on its own. Imagine travel books that focus only on the logistics of travel and never narrate the sights and sounds of new places. Imagine astronomers so fascinated by their telescopes they never aim them at actual stars. Imagine chefs who debate and edit recipes without preparing and then sharing and reveling in actual meals.

If the heart of what education is about—the meals, the stars, the travel experience—is missing from too many books about school, it's no wonder creative people balk at entering the profession. Already low in status, relatively modest in pay, why would anyone embrace what Frank McCourt called the "downstairs maid of the professions"?

This book is a quiet alternative to those narratives about schools. It's a celebration of what it is to be a teacher. It's for the people already showing up every day to give their best to students. It's for anyone considering joining those unheralded ranks. It's a "why do" this work—not another "how to."

I started this project after twenty years in the classroom. Throughout those decades, I noticed something poignant over and over: when I spoke to other people about school or about education, their reactions were tired or cynical. But when I started asking people to tell me about a formative teacher, or an important teacher, or a favorite teacher, it was a whole different ballgame. I still do this. People light up and lean forward. They're eager to relate what an eighth-grade English teacher or a tenth-grade math teacher did to change their life. The accounts are inspiring, and almost everybody has one. I know I do. Books about teaching, books about schools need to capture some of that love, that beauty, that inspiration, that heart. We have too many telescopes and not enough stars.

I have a personal stake in this too, as the book's structure makes clear. *Teaching Life* begins with a letter to my daughters, one a graduate student determined to join the teaching ranks, the other, as I write, already starting her first job with Teach for America. I am, in a way, cheering them both on as I think about what this work involves. I'm thinking of what it will mean for them to be happy and successful in whatever teaching worlds they end up in, and for however long. If the best young minds (and my daughters count as that) are to be attracted to this profession, teaching has to seem to be the artistry it is. It should be seen as a privilege to be a teacher. It should be like working for Doctors Without Borders. *Teaching Life* is my modest contribution to that ennobling.

The world our students are inheriting is only growing more complex and uncertain. The speed of change is dizzying. When I started teaching, I still used chalk on a blackboard, and the whole world, as the Cold War thawed, was assumed to be on a fast track toward democracy—the only game in town. We did not Google because there was no Google, and our little flip phones only made calls. I had this book fully drafted when Covid-19 hit and threw a generational challenge at schools, making seasoned teachers feel like rookies all over again. I had this book drafted when the killing of George Floyd raised questions also about how schools were addressing racism and inequities, making us all attend to blind spots and biases. How to build sturdy school life when the landscape moves so quickly? How to equip students when you can't see what lies ahead of them?

I add this book to the crowded field of books about education because I think the best way to encourage and sustain great schools is by attracting and nourishing great teachers, and the best way to multiply great teachers is to name what they do and then value what they do so highly that other people with talent and heart and vision and life will want to do it too. It's not the only thing we need. I don't pretend this book is an exhaustive blueprint for forward-thinking schools. But having the very best people in classrooms is indispensable to whatever the right forward-thinking program turns out to be.

For two and half decades now, I have been inspired over and over by colleagues in classrooms. Great teachers are remarkable to witness. Teaching really is an art form. But there are no galleries to display the real work of a teacher—their students are their gallery—there are no teacher-stages for crowds to gather in front of, no college-style video Great Courses singling out prominent practitioners. It is patient, unsung work. For their sake, and for our schools, I want to sing it here.

LESSON 1

WHAT TEACHING IS FOR

*It is ominous, a presumption of crime, that this word
Education has so cold, so hopeless a sound. A treatise on
education, a convention for education, a lecture, a system,
affects us with slight paralysis and a certain yawning of
the jaws.*

— Emerson

Dear Katie and Emily:

I know one of you has been thinking hard about teaching as a
career for a long time now, and the other has dived right into
the classroom after college. With two parents in the
profession, you were destined, or doomed, to at least consider
this work! I'm all for it, even though, over the years, when
I've told people what I do, the responses range from "thank
you for your service" to "better you than me."

When I sat down to write this, I wasn't thinking about
advice so much as vista, vantage. I want you both to see what
the profession can be, at its best, and so to think of your
relationship to what it is—before you get swept up in the
frenzy of the days. That's my bias, I suppose, for an examined
life. At any rate, plenty of people can show you the ropes of
the daily work: how to organize and manage a class, how to
give feedback, how to run a meeting with parents, how to
design units and collaborate with colleagues. All that. It's

hard, and it's the work, and I'm not downplaying it at all, but I'm going to stay big and broad here. I want to help you think about the why and the what first, not the how. And while I began with you in mind and determined to tell you everything relevant I think I've learned in my more than twenty years of teaching, I ended up thinking about my colleagues too, and everybody else in your shoes considering the craft, and all the parents of students we all teach who could use a reminder about what we're really trying to do in school, and to administrators, who make or break a school with the priorities they focus on. And I want to clarify up front that these are my reflections about teaching not about education. I'm not equipped to make policy pronouncements. My experiences are too narrow for that, my biography too small. Also, I've grown tired of books about schools (and other things) that sound like jeremiads rather than poetry. Not that I don't think there are good fights to be joined, just that that's not what I'm setting out to do here. As Dante put it: not the flight for these particular wings. My gray-haired preference is for something that affirms. Read lots of other perspectives, tap other sources of expertise. Take what you will from this one, then read everything else you can. The best teachers have a polymath streak and are tireless lifelong learners. Let this be one of a thousand points of view you absorb as you form your own.

I didn't attend great schools growing up. I think you two probably know this. But I did have a few crucial teachers. The most important one I ever had was an eleventh-grade English teacher who wore a sweater over her shoulders, rarely left her stool at the front of the room, never raised her voice, was as methodical as a nurse, but who changed my life nonetheless by recognizing that something was stirring in me because of the novels we were reading in her class. She saw something happening, and she gave it space and encouragement. In the small mountain town where I grew up, far from universities and museums, a middle-aged, unmarried graduate of Radford

College, Ms. Acuff, loaned me books, suggested writers I might read, pointed me to a store downtown that sold stationery and greeting cards and figurines, but also, off to one side, two cases of literary books that were different from the books at B. Dalton's at the mall. You had to walk behind the cash register to even access the shelves. I bought my first John Updike and Philip Roth novels there. I bought a collection of poems by E.E. Cummings. I bought a paperback of *Crime and Punishment* that I still have on a shelf, list price 75 cents, an impressionistic Raskolnikov face on the cover. I got those books because of Ms. Acuff. She paid attention to me and saw something like curiosity, like life, going on in my young mind, and she nourished it with knowledge I didn't have about what to do with whatever it was that was quickening inside. She changed my life without getting off her stool.

My history teacher that same year, Mr. Mitchell, couldn't have been more different. He was an old-school lecturer so entertaining—and forbidding—students never interrupted him with questions. He didn't invite questions either. When we walked into class, he would be busy writing an exhaustive outline on the board—he filled two walls of boards with notes—then he would go down the hall to get a drink of water while we copied what he'd written, and when he came back he would start lecturing and not stop until the bell rang. Unless we were taking a test, every day was exactly the same. Nothing like the student-centered way we're told to teach now. I remember hearing the audio of filmstrips playing in the adjacent history room, but we never watched filmstrips in our class. Mr. Mitchell had too much to say. He spent summer vacations visiting historical sites and would tell stories about his travels. He mined biographies for quirky facts, reveled in presidential nicknames like Old Kinderhook (Martin Van Buren) and Ruther*fraud* B. Hayes. He loved the military and hoped his son would go to one of the academies. In the mountain South, almost everyone was religious, and in our tax-payer-funded public school, Mr. Mitchell didn't hesitate to talk about "the precious blood of our Lord and Savior Jesus Christ." We spent close to a month studying— that is, listening to him talk about—the Civil War. The Battle of Chancellorsville, where Stonewall Jackson was critically wounded, still made Mr. Mitchell, after all these years describing it, go solemn. He loved history, and for all the blind spots and missed perspectives I recognize now, his passion, and his person, his personality, his life, still live in my memory. He was fully inside whatever subject he lectured on, but when you spoke with him one on one he didn't look you directly in the eye, and his neck, I remember, from collar to jaw, was covered with a razor burn that made him seem vulnerable, even hurt. He wore short-sleeved dress shirts and the era's wide ties. He gave back tests high grade to low, so that you always knew who had conquered, who had bombed.

How vivid these formative teachers remain. I loved Mr. Mitchell, and your grandmother always thought he was the teacher who changed my life because I would talk about him, but it was Ms. Acuff, quietly holding me back after class, who did the deeper work. It was Ms. Acuff who, when I went back in my forties to speak at a local college, I invited because I wanted to pay tribute to her publicly and did. Working on this book, I looked her up on the internet and was devastated to discover her obituary and thought there could be no other student of her hundreds and hundreds of students who could possibly be as grateful or as grief-stricken as I was. And it's interesting to me that I, who am such a sucker for the larger-than-life figure, full of quirk, claim as my most important teacher someone calm and quiet as Walden Pond.

When I celebrate transformational teaching in the pages to come, I'm not thinking of a single type of charisma. Not every class has to be the *Dead Poets Society*—not many of them should be! I never tried to be Mr. Mitchell; you probably really shouldn't stand on your desk like Robin Williams (though I *have* walked on tables while reading a poem by Billy

Collins). Also, not every teacher has to inspire every kid. So, free yourself of that pressure. But somewhere along the line, all students should encounter someone who rearranges things and sets them on a path, and in an ideal world schools would be filled with teams of teachers who consider themselves a community existing to do just that. Some kids will be mobilized by you; others by the teacher across the hall who you don't even maybe get along with all that well. I never saw Mr. Mitchell and Ms. Acuff exchange a word—not once! Inspiration is quiet teamwork, and while it's not the job description in full, being a teacher filled with life who inspires life in students seems to me the condition of everything else we want school to be. Until interest and life have been mobilized, we're orchestrating activity but not yet really educating. Great teachers are filled with purpose and joy. They themselves are alive to something, and it's infectious with their students. And that's how transformation begins.

One thing that nags anyone thinking of teaching below the college level, and one thing you need to stare down from the outset, is the status of the job—or the perception of low status. A fairly recent book called *The Teacher Wars* by Dana Goldstein is a compelling history of the profession in America. Add it to your list. I assume you're keeping a list of things you want to read someday? At your age you should still want to try to read almost everything. When you get to my age, what you'll want instead is to reread a few big things—and take walks on the beach. (Come visit me.)

Anyway, I'm of two minds about the question of status. One the one hand, it shouldn't matter. Those of us who teach know the rewards are different: they're personal, emotional, and lasting. I taught with someone who was a television producer until he came to our school. His father was a teacher, and my colleague had gone to his retirement party and heard all these accounts of what his father had done, what his impact was, and he decided nobody was going to pay those kinds of tributes to him in the work he was in. He's teaching now, this former producer. Another colleague told me at lunch one day that he received an email from a former student who is teaching in Mongolia. He had written a long note to say how my colleague had changed his life in 10th grade. "What did you do for him?" I asked. "I watched him," my colleague said. "For several months I watched him, then I figured something out about him, and I named it for him. Then I said, because you're *that*, you should think about trying *this*." And there was the magic. He saw something, and then he used what he saw to provoke something else. And now that kid is off in Mongolia recalling it. "What do you think you did?" I asked my colleague. "He had it inside him," he said. "But when I saw it and named it, that pulled it out into the open where he could see it too." Relationships and encounters—people and experiences—are always the foundation of great teaching. And as infuriating and repetitive as the days can be, those rewards really do compensate for the lack of larger status the profession deserves.

Having said that, I'm jealous for the profession too. It shouldn't be seen as a second family-income job, supplementing the breadwinner. It often is. It shouldn't be the case that teachers who need to make more money have to look to become administrators. The number of teachers I know who tutor for extra money would astonish you. I did it one year too. I needed the money. And when we lived in North Carolina, I taught every summer at a program for rising high school seniors, and that was car-repair money, or that set of new tires we needed, or birthday-present money, or unexpected-dentist-bill money. Teaching shouldn't be a fallback for people who decide *real* academic work is not for them. Be wary of trying to teach up, by the way. If you want to teach college kids, become a professor. Don't teach high school kids like it's college. If you teach middle school, don't envy the high school teacher. Give yourself to the students you have. Don't teach up.

And while it's ridiculous to be consoled by this, for what

it's worth, here are some heavyweights who spent time teaching below the college level: Nietzsche, Wittgenstein, Sartre, Simone de Beauvoir, D.H. Lawrence, Vincent van Gogh, Mary Wollstonecraft, Charlotte Bronte, Louisa May Alcott, Walt Whitman, Herman Melville, Countee Cullen, James Baldwin, Agnes Martin, Lyndon Johnson, Tolstoy, Thoreau, Roberta Flack! Pretty good company.

I'm not sure exactly how the two of you are thinking about it. I was one of those people who backed into teaching. I didn't have a vision for it at first; I just thought I might be good at it. It didn't instantly transform as a calling either. The way I'm writing about it here *is* a vision, but it took years for that to form. I think that's one reason I'm writing this now. I want people in your shoes to see what the work really is and what it can be, because once you're in it, it can be like riding a bicycle in front of a fire engine just to keep up with daily demands. Before you begin, make sure you've at least asked the big questions: What is teaching really about? What are we trying to do every day when we stand in front of students? Why are we there, and what are we hoping for? Too many people answer these questions small. They imagine themselves as bricklayers with no conception of what's being built. Their job, as they see it, is to mortar one brick on top of another and keep their head down. They are not building monuments or cathedrals. They're laying bricks. I suspect most are content for the people above them somewhere to have the answers, to know the design, to be able to say how each bricklaying task is part of something larger. And those borrowed answers are often wildly inadequate and uninspiring. They usually involve filling student toolkits with skills. That's usually the extent of it. That and preparing students for the next level of work—what John Dewey dismissed as "mere preparation." More on that later. And you can't know what a school or a classroom is for unless you have some sense in yourself of what a life is for. So, take your time figuring that out as you launch. What I'm hoping to do here is to help you think about this profession as an art form, as a vision thrumming with life, so that you're not one of those who answers questions about teaching too small.

Before I spend all my energy on that cause, I owe it to you raise a question and maybe even some doubts. Certainly, if you listen to policy debates and read articles and books about the direction of education, you won't recognize your father's credo and you won't encounter the word inspiration very often at all. Instead, you'll encounter words like standards and skills, assessments and accountabilities. These aren't insidious. Part of the job is absolutely holding students accountable for learning and being yourself accountable for their growth. I'm not advocating a free-for-all educational community in which Romantic teachers do whatever feels best to them, and students are magically, mystically transformed. It never feels like that. Students should be asked to do hard things, even things they don't want to do at all.

A lot of the time, even if your commitments sound like Emerson, your days will feel like a traffic cop's. Teaching is hard and exhausting. There's a reason talented people walk away. Every day it's like the starter's pistol firing, and from the moment students start walking through the door until the last one leaves, you're *on*: performing, parenting, intuiting, assessing, collaborating, creating, redirecting, corralling. And then you have papers to grade and meetings to attend, and you take work home, and the whole thing starts all over again the next morning. That's the demoralizing part. It keeps coming at you. You spend a week grading a big stack of papers then groan inside when you give a next assignment that will repeat the load for the following week. And so on. It's Sisyphean. And you can't really have a down day because your students go on showing up. You will almost certainly barely have time to eat lunch. You might struggle for enough passing privacy to make a phone call to your doctor. Parents will sometimes call administrators to complain about things their kids said you did or didn't do, or, because they went to school and so know something about the job second-hand, don't hesitate to challenge your decisions or approaches. I've had parents chide my teaching choices by referring to the great teacher their kid had *before* me at another school. It can be too much. A colleague admits she called home every night her first-year teaching just to get a pep talk from her family. I still see myself my first year on the job, books spread all over the spare bedroom of our first apartment (beside the crib each of you used), working on weekends to stay exactly one week ahead of my three preps—and doing it again the next weekend. A mound of work a week at a time. I had a colleague once who had to stand up at a parent-teacher conference and ask a father to leave; he was being that rude. I had another friend who had to pull the activity bus over on the shoulder of an interstate to quiet students down— because she was the only adult on the bus. My own humanities team and I were rebuked by a security guard at the Metropolitan Museum of Art because a few of our kids could not follow directions and control themselves, much less be inspired by "The Death of Socrates." Read Frank McCourt's memoir *Teacher Man* for a dozen other indignities. The job burns people out for good reasons.

But it also inspires. Well into my fifties now, I remain committed to Emerson's ideal that the goal of education should be "commensurate with the goal of life." An ambiguity flows out of this claim that is encouraging, at least to me: Why should education have ground rules of certainty that the rest of our life doesn't offer? And if we're equipping students for the life in front of them, not for tests we think prove certain achievements, why shouldn't school have the same dynamic of trial and error, hesitation, experiment, and varieties of feedback that our actual life does? And why, if we want our life to be animated with passion and curiosity and interest and accomplishment, should school be anything other than the first draft of that? Why teach recipes without preparing meals? Schools should be full of feeling and variety and curiosity and challenges and community because that's what the world can feel like. If school were a smaller part of a young person's life, it might be forgivable to focus on the transmission of key skills. But since school, for students, is a full-time job plus daily work to take home, stretching across a dozen and more formative years, it should be worthy of all the time and attention we ask of them. It shouldn't be what students too often experience it as: a placeholder, mere preparation, awaiting the real life to come. School should do what Tolstoy said art should do: *make people love life*.

If school shouldn't be boring, books about school shouldn't be either. If the condition of great teaching is, as I'm insisting, vitality and its incitement, then writing about school can't afford to be lifeless. Books about love might focus on the biochemistry of the thing, or the evolution of the thing, or the cultural determinants of the thing, but at some point we need poets and novelists and songwriters— and everyday people in love—to give us the thing itself. School also has a *thing itself*, and it's not reducible to data or curriculum or policy. That thing itself is probably best captured in portraits and stories.

And so, remarkable children of mine, I'm thinking about you in the context of all these mediations on teaching. If thinking about what I would say to you as you head down this path has me also thinking of others, you sparked the idea, and, anyway, if it doesn't help you, I don't imagine it will help anyone else. And while I won't veer off to truly personal advice or elaborate on how proud I am of you both or call you by your nicknames in front of everyone who stumbles across these reflections, even beginning to write this makes me remember you both young. I used to say to one of you, stop growing up so fast! You always replied, I can't help it, as if I were missing the most obvious thing in the world. I remember picking one of you up from your first day at preschool. You had your fingers in your mouth, and you were clinging to Ms. Lenora's long summer skirt. Right, Ms.

Lenora? I remember dropping one of you off for your first day of kindergarten. The principal scolded me for getting out of the car to shoot video. You're holding up the drop-off line, she said sternly. I'm a teacher, I wanted to fire back, claiming professional solidarity—but I didn't. On the last day of kindergarten for the other of you, I got my video camera out to record the milestone. What was your favorite thing this year? I asked. The work, you said. I tried to press you for details. What about the work, what part of it? I asked. You got sad more than upset, as if I'd hurt your feelings. Just, the work, you said, holding back your patient tears. In college, you both sought out ways to travel overseas, full of curiosity and fearlessness. One of you texted me once: my school is sponsoring a trip to the opera in New York; I'll be bored, right, but I should go, right, to see the Met? You went. The other of you went in quest of the Great Barrier Reef, before, you told me, it's not there to see. People often think younger generations are knowing and cool, but you two have wonder and warmth. I'm dizzily proud of you.

And since we dragged in the Met, I'll close my introduction with this: One Christmas a few years back, I attended a performance of Bach's Brandenburg Concertos at Lincoln Center. It was one of the best things I've ever done. The music itself was magical, but it was also that the performers were so exuberant, so committed to the piece. Occasionally one of the violinists almost leapt, going up on one foot like Cupid. Another turned his body back and forth like a matador. Two violinists, facing off in musical conversation, nodded tribute to each other at movement's end, while the audience applauded. And it felt like the answer to a thousand tough questions I couldn't quite articulate. Greatness. Artistry. Inspiration. Lift. This book is my argument that teaching can achieve something like that too.

FIRST THINGS FIRST

In order that teachers may delight in awakening the spirits of children, they must themselves be awake.

— Ella Flagg Young, retiring as Chicago
superintendent of schools, Jan. 1, 1916

Here's a story that won't seem to mean much on its own but that shows very quietly one of the great foundational things teachers do all the time. It may be the most important of all.

I was teaching seventh-grade history at an independent school near Raleigh, North Carolina, and it was the first day of the new year. After fourth period, my colleague and I were out in the hall, monitoring the crowd. It was time to go to lunch, and students everywhere, released from the surrounding rooms, were shoving their bags and books into their lockers so they could get to the cafeteria as fast as possible. About a hundred of them were crowded in the space. Another hundred eighth-graders at the far end of the hall would vie for the same central staircase. And there was an air of excitement because it was the first day back and this was the first chance all day for students to organize themselves and be with who they wanted to be. My colleague Toby and I, monitoring them idly, were making our own quiet survey: What hand had we been dealt this time? Which of the kids darting around the common space would prove to be classroom leaders and stars? Which ones would be upstarts? Any siblings of former students here? Which was the kid we all knew by name because the 6th grade teachers had told us how unreasonable his mother could be, though the kid was lovely? And then, as we stood there talking, we saw one of the new students, Kevin, standing by himself in the gathering crowd. Kevin wasn't in any distress, but he did look lost, and so my colleague left me and went over to make sure this new kid knew that lunch was next. I followed behind. Do you know how to get to the cafeteria? Toby asked. Kevin said he wasn't sure. Well, I'm going there now, Toby said. Come on. Let's walk together.

Moving with the loud, manic crowd, I watched Toby talking to Kevin along the way: down the stairwell, outside by the field where the middle school kids improvised games during break, up to the cafeteria in its building by the gym. Toby steered Kevin to the food line inside, then he left him and went over to his own assigned table to supervise a group of ten kids and ask them, no doubt, about their summer. That was all. First-day-back stuff for teachers everywhere. The kind of thing you just do every day that no one has to tell you to do. The kind of thing that isn't in any orientation binder. Watching kids, noticing them, and making quiet moves in response.

I taught Kevin world history that year and worked with him for another year in a video editing club. He was pleasant, motivated, and well adjusted, and in the course of things, he moved on to the high school on the other side of our campus, and other seventh-graders claimed our attention. Toby and I still saw Kevin occasionally, though. He was a kid who, without being at the center of main social circles, had a lot of optimism and charm regardless. One way to measure teenagers' maturity, I often think, is to watch them interact with adults. If they do that well, if they shift to that mode, if they speak confidently and politely with teachers and the parents of their friends, it means they know themselves, or are beginning to know themselves reasonably well—comfortable in their own skin. In high school, Kevin had all that. His big extracurricular was the student news broadcast; he kept up his work in video. When I saw him his senior year, broadcast journalism was what he hoped to major in at college.

One of the things the seniors did at our school was compile recollections and memories in books that were displayed in the library in the weeks before graduation. Half a decade after his first day at our school, Kevin began his section with a description of how, on that first day, when he didn't know where to go for lunch, a teacher had suggested they walk together, and along the way the teacher and he had a simple conversation, and then they went inside the cafeteria and that was all. End of gesture. But across these formative years, it left an impression. A kid on the brink of going out into the world, it still meant something to him that an adult in the building didn't let him feel lost in his new surroundings.

Years after the fact, Kevin never forgot what my colleague did. It seems so obvious to do, and yet it's so easy to ignore. This attention to the personal. This looking-out for kids. This noticing of what is going on. The eye for what matters. The simplicity of just seeing things and caring about them is the beginning of everything else in the teaching life. It takes instinct but it also takes a certain mindset. In this mode, you are not playing defense or trying to avoid mistakes and not miss things on a teacher checklist. You are open to what the students in front of you are and need. You realize that while your job involves a lot of lessons and assessments and curriculum, these encounters with students are your vocation, and so you remain open to those encounters and you follow them and even cultivate them, prioritizing them whenever they appear. It's a kind of orientation to the work that lets you see that lost new kid as the most important thing in your teaching world at that moment.

Virginia Woolf once praised the whole era of Elizabethan writers—Shakespeare and Co.—for having a kind of inner freedom: "They seem to have an attitude to life," she writes, "a position which allows them to move their limbs freely; a view, which, though made up of all sorts of different things, falls into the right perspective for their purposes." She goes on: "They had an attitude to life which made them able to express themselves freely and fully. Shakespeare's plays are not the work of a baffled and frustrated mind; they are the perfectly elastic envelope of his thought."

I love that idea about literature. I also love the idea that there's a kind of freedom at the heart of teaching too, and it might be the right place to begin thinking about a job that can be both baffling and frustrating. Shakespeare, it goes without saying, didn't have to take attendance five times a day and sit through weekly faculty meetings. And his actors all wanted to be there, I presume. But what Woolf admires is Shakespeare's "attitude to life." Above everything else, it seems to me, teachers, similarly, need a feeling for the life of their students. With that in place, they become available to the moment and the need. Their heads are up. They are seeing what there is to see. They are open to encounters.

In the movie *October Sky*, a high school kid named Homer grows up in a coal mining community and, in those long-ago Sputnik days, becomes obsessed with rockets (the movie is based on a book called *Rocket Boys*). Homer's father, a foreman at the mines, opposes what he sees as Homer's distractions and nonsense. The West Virginia world the movie inhabits has seemingly three concerns only: coal, football, and traditional family life. But Homer has other ideas. In the center of his existential drama, there is, of course, a teacher, this one played by Laura Dern, who recognizes what he's after—she notices what's going on in him the way my colleague saw what was happening with Kevin that day. And she did the simple life-changing thing that so many teachers do: she recognized and named it, and, pointing him to a science competition, helped steer Homer in this unfamiliar direction.

And note that we're not even talking about classrooms yet. We haven't even really begun. We're out in the hallway, watching kids like Kevin, in a fairly new school near Raleigh, North Carolina. In the display case is a poster welcoming students back, and on the shelves are pictures of all the seventh-grade teachers when they were in seventh grade, and the students are supposed to guess who is who, because the teachers want to show students—and remind themselves— that they once wore seventh-grade shoes too, and they pinched, because those younger teacher selves felt a little unsure, and also looked around for friends—these teachers, who've spent basically their whole life inside schools, and whose students remind them over and over that they were young, and in many ways, maybe, still are. In the hall now, actual kids are pouring out of classrooms. Small groups of students are huddling to share secrets and catch up. Others are jumping on each other's backpacks. Again. Students, a teacher standing in her classroom doorway calls. And how much of a teacher's life is spent watching students from a doorway! This teacher calls out other unnecessary instructions, because what she's really doing is reminding the hundred seventh-graders that a boundary exists, that a teacher is here, and somehow, wonderfully, if precariously, that has an effect, and the space stays safe enough, and the kids are okay even as their hundred unique biographies roil beneath the dozens of throwaway conversations and the unspoken anxiety to be liked and be part of some group, any group. And in the rush of students closing lockers and hurrying away, that new kid looks up, looks around, without distress, but clearly confused, and a teacher tells another he'll catch up with him later, then goes to the new kid, and they walk on together, and it's the world's simplest thing, and it went completely unnoticed until Kevin sat down to think, six years later, about what made his time at the school so meaningful.

THE TORTOISE AND THE HARE

*The closest I can come is to say it was something in the
air—or something not in the air. Mr. Bowler's
classroom always felt fresh, as if the windows had been
open a long time. There was no staleness or tension, no
emotion or expectation emanating from him to sully the
atmosphere. We walked in with no balance sheet
appended to our names; and just as we produced the
proof of the day out of nothing, so we ourselves came into
being as if for the first time.*

— Jane Tompkins, *A Life in School*

At the North Carolina school where I taught for fourteen
years, we divided our 7th grade world history class into four
main units, beginning with the Dark Ages, which, because
our own new millennium was turning, we centered on the
year 1000. To take advantage of the mania about Y2K
computer bugs, we billed a culminating Dark Age
marketplace the Y1K Festival. It became a signature part of
the 7th grade experience, and over the years it got more and
more elaborate. Students wore period costumes and set their
booths up in a small courtyard to simulate a bazaar. We had a
festival currency that parents spent to buy historical goods.
The local newspaper ran a story on us once. And one year we
got permission to bring in a camel to stand at the edge of the
marketplace. When word got out about that, upper school

students poured down to see it. My colleagues joked that we would have to leave now, after the year of the camel, because there was no other way for us to do more with Y1K.

The whole project became a finely oiled machine. A team of teachers had it all down. Students spent six weeks considering historical case studies together, even as they did research on their own specific country or Dark Age culture. We required a major piece of writing. We filled in and illustrated trade and travel maps. We made Dark Age mortar using an old Russian recipe and had a contest to see whose mortar could hold bricks. We played an online Viking conquest game. We did research twice a week for a month. Finally, having written an argument paper, each student had to pass an oral interview about their culture. We also gave a very traditional unit test on the things we'd studied in common. Convinced our foundational work was solid, we turned our attention to organizing the festival. And here, every year—it happened like clockwork—was when we used to say the school year really began, on a late September day, in week seven or so of school, the weather still warm with late southern summer, when students, all the papers and interviews and graded tests returned, would come to classes and for several days work together on the festival itself.

There was a lot to do in a short period of time. We issued programs to parents, and those had to be printed and folded. We stuffed each program with an initial batch of Y1K currency (modeled after medieval Chinese huizis); those "bills" had to be printed, cut, and compiled—different color paper for different denominations. We needed to borrow paper cutters from art classes. We needed a sign for the Y1K "bank." We had tri-fold boards for displaying information about the cultures; those had to be designed and pasted with materials.

And so, for several days if you walked into our classrooms at the north end of the second floor of the middle school

building at Cary Academy in Cary, North Carolina, you would
see groups of seventh-graders doing all manner of tasks in
very messy spaces. Tri-folds would be everywhere. On the
front tables, groups of students and teachers are cutting
huizis very carefully with cutting boards and scissors. We
assign students to be quality control. One sheet of huizis
done well, we tell students, is better than a hundred done fast.
Take your time. Details matter. Over there, other students are
folding programs. Astonishingly, they have to learn how to
do this. So, we learn how to fold something straight together.
At some point, we teachers are making laps around the
rooms, inspecting tri-folds, offering praise and anticipation,
or telling a group they have a great idea but that their
overview of the Vikings has misspelled words, and could they
see if they can find them, correct them, and reprint. To one
side, two girls have brought in a small bolt of purple cloth.
They're making tunics for themselves, using simple
instructions they found online. Glue sticks are everywhere,
the caps shipwrecked on the floor. A few kids, ahead of the
game, are organizing PowerPoint presentations on their
laptops. They also want to play Byzantine music through their
computer. Is that okay? More than okay, we tell them.
Everyone's central writing piece is part of the display. In an
email and in our welcome on the day itself, we'll tell parents
to ask students: *Was* your culture in a Dark Age? Is this a fair
historical description of that place in that time? What's the
argument you made? Over there, some boys with needle-nose
pliers are bending metal wire to make chainmail. Another
student is doing something with glitter. Why glitter? we ask.
Because Ghana traded gold, she says. Teachers settle back at
the table up front. How are we doing? we ask, admiring the
piles of huizis. We stack them in an empty Hammermill paper
box. A student gives us the count. We grab scissors too. On a
teacher desk, inspired by the recent Ken Burns documentary
on jazz, we are playing a John Coltrane CD. And as we cut
huizis, we talk, sometimes about Y1K, more often about
other things: families, fall break plans, how 7th grade is going

so far, how 7th grade is different from 6th grade, or the same, what the best lunch is, what their older siblings did when they had Y1K—whatever, it doesn't matter what the topic is. Some student always asks us, what if it rains? Parents ask this too. It never rains on Y1K, we tell them. Yeah, but what if it does? the student repeats. It's Y1K, we say. It never rains. How do you grade our festival? someone asks. It's hard to, we say. Yeah, but how will you grade it? What do you think the best way to assess all this work would be? we ask them. Can we all get A's? the student asks. You *can* all get A's, of course, we say. Is that really what you're worried about? Not really, the student says. The main thing now, we say, is to step into it. Have fun, but really engage the visitors. Don't wait for them to show interest. Make them interested. You've done great work. Trust your preparation and have fun with this. But what if it rains? a different student says.

It was the beginning of the school year for me every time, because having done some hard initial work together, intellectual work, research work, a formal paper, now we're taking our time folding programs and cutting currency or making tunics, and everyone is doing something, and the teachers are a close-knit team, and everybody's students are everybody else's, and the music is the locomotive urging us on, and we're talking, as if we're making a huge quilt and everyone is sewing their square, and we have no real agenda for the conversation, and we learn about our students, and they relax but stay on task, and we become something other than we were. Every time.

And here's the thing: we couldn't have begun the year like that. We needed the six weeks of hard work first. This had to come on the far side of that work. The hard work gave us purpose. It said, we're trying to understand some important things and learn how to speak about them critically but also creatively. *That's* what we're doing. And then, lo and behold, by doing that hard work and then changing up the order, shifting the dynamic, making what had been formal feel informal, even familial, filling silent space with some jazz, we were suddenly the group we would be for the rest of the year. We somehow found each other. We hadn't orchestrated the project to do this, but over the years it became obvious that that was the most meaningful byproduct of what we did. Had you walked in on us you might have seen frenzy—and mess. If you'd been with us all along for the first stretch of academic work, you would have seen calm, and you may have sensed something vital and transformational in the room the way I did every year. The students seemed to own their work. We owned it, all of us, together. And then one year, we brought in a camel.

In Max Steele's short story "The Cat and the Coffee Drinkers," an eccentric small-town teacher gathers a select group of students to her private kindergarten to teach them how to read. That's what she's known for. But she doesn't begin with reading. She begins with teaching them how to sweep and dust and clean windows and say their name confidently, then how to use a false name confidently because that could be useful too. She teaches them about her no-good cat Mr. Thomas, she teaches them how to drink coffee, and she teaches them, as she says, about rooms, because we spend most of our lives in rooms and don't really pay attention to them. Only in November, Steele writes, did they "settle down to the real work that gave Miss Effie's kindergarten its reputation. Reading. Miss Effie liked to read, and it was well known in the town and especially among the public-school teachers that the two or three hundred children she had taught had grown up reading everything they could find."

I love this story for all kinds of reasons. We used to read it to our 7th grade students every winter. At the end of the story, I marvel at how high the stakes become, and how moving, when Miss Effie decides the class needs to help her put down her wounded cat. And I'm taken by her idiosyncrasies throughout (our students were always confused about why she gave coffee to kindergartners); I love her southern spinster crankiness. And I love the way she waits to teach reading, and understands that all the early work sweeping and learning about coffee is groundwork for the reading, because she is building a space around them, a habitat for the learning, and that space, that atmosphere, that style, those conditions establish how they will be together for a while. Then they read.

Teachers like Miss Effie are as patient with students as they are impatient with frozen schemes. They're defiant toward the hares who want to sprint from thing to thing, covering material, filling toolkits, preparing for next things. Inside their classrooms, they are tortoises, these great teachers, some of them quiet, some of them loud and charismatic. But they turtle along because they've learned to see what Emerson reminded us to hold onto: something else is doing the real work. The teacher is instigator, facilitator, gardener, you name it. The change and the inspiration occur inside the student, where nature does exactly what it will, when it will. What you want is to create optimal conditions for that growth. It took me years to learn this. It took me years to realize I wasn't doing the work. I was facilitating it. It took me years to trust that tending to those conditions for growth could involve very incidental, seemingly insignificant tasks, especially if you could somehow make them personal: room-sweeping, for example, before reading by a stove; or fake-currency cutting—paper scraps everywhere—to the sounds of "Love Supreme."

DIOGENES

There is no more light in a genius than in any other honest man—but he has a particular kind of lens to concentrate this light into a burning point.
— Wittgenstein, *Culture and Value*

Before I decided to become a teacher, I attended Princeton Seminary. This was in the mid-1990s—the Clinton years— and the small student body organized itself informally but unmistakably into camps. There was a robust group of diehard evangelicals. There were people whose main passion was social justice. There was an interesting group of second-career students, accomplished in previous fields and now looking for a life change, including my friend Larry, who had fought in Vietnam, been an investment banker in New York, built his own house from scratch, and now was looking to serve in a church. There were people interested in the academic study of religion. And there were students like me who had come out of fairly intense religious experiences and were looking for a new way to think about themselves and the world without renouncing religion itself outright. For each of these groups there was a faculty member who was a kind of guru or guiding light. I can still name the professors most beloved by these different camps.

My own most important seminary professor was an idiosyncratic philosophy teacher so aptly named Diogenes you will decide I am making it up—I am not—whose following straddled two camps: the diehard evangelicals and those who used to be evangelical. I heard about him before I ever walked into his class. He was the kind of professor who wanted to weed out people who weren't utterly serious about what he was teaching. He wasn't there to give you some equipment for your ministry. He was there to challenge the way you thought and not to hold your hand and make you feel good for trying your best. He was a tough grader, and he didn't suffer fools, but, people said, the students who signed up for his classes tended to take them all—Diogenes devotees. I became one for a while.

His Philosophy of Religion course met in a ground-floor room in a stout Romanesque building at the corner of the seminary quad. He came into class wearing a wool jacket, gray wool pants, and a dark tie. His appearance was British, and I still think sometimes when I wear essentially the same arrangement of woolen items to teach in that I'm imitating or paying loose tribute to Diogenes. He didn't ask us our names that first day. He didn't ask why we'd signed up for this course. He didn't ask us what kind of philosophical backgrounds we had. He didn't go over a syllabus. He didn't ask us what we hoped for from his class. Instead, he announced and launched the main work we were going to take on. It was like a ship releasing from the harbor. The ropes fell fast. We were going to read one book very carefully, Diogenes said, and for as long as it took until we understood it deeply. We don't read with enough care anymore, he went on. And what followed was the first of so many seemingly free-flowing stream-of-consciousness meditations, as if he were praying aloud but with great frustration. We're in a hurry to read every damn book on the shelves, he said. I used to teach an entire class on Plato's *Republic*. That's all we read. I might do that again sometime, who knows? Or, *The*

Symposium. We think we know more than Plato now. We don't bother to read him. We know the critiques. We know all his blind spots. But it's not a question of knowledge really, is it? Diogenes pressed. And he leaned forward over his wooden lectern to address us, and his eyebrows twitched as he spoke. What did Jesus want from us? Not what do you *know*, you see, but what do you, what? He paused, but no one answered. No one dared speak. We weren't sure how to speak with him yet. He didn't care. He went on, not quite in a trance, but in a zone—flow. What do you *treasure*? he said. That's why Kierkegaard used to go down to the main church in Copenhagen and sit on the steps reading a newspaper while the service let out. Because people in church were like ducks, you see, shouting together, we can fly, we can fly, then they do what? They waddle back out of church again and waddle down the street. That's why Nietzsche said of Christians not, they need better theology, but, what? Diogenes paused for more silence, then went on. They need to sing better hymns.

He was off, and in my memory, warped by affection and nostalgia and admiration, he didn't stop this free play of associations until the course ended. And he did walk us methodically through that one book—Hume's *Dialogues Concerning Natural Religion*—but honestly that felt like a catalyst to wind up Diogenes' ranging mind to go wherever it wanted. I used to scrawl his off-hand comments in my notebooks with more fury than I recorded main ideas. One of my favorites went like this: "Pascal was smart. Smarter than Paul." Paul the Apostle credited with writing most of the New Testament. "Wittgenstein was a *lot* smarter than Paul," Diogenes went on. Then, getting excited, as if he'd just remembered this man: "Leibniz was a *hell* of a lot smarter than Paul. But the difference is, what? Kierkegaard taught us. It's the difference between a genius and an apostle." Once, he was talking about cosmology, and he referred to "that Hawking fellow." I'm smiling to write that and recall it, though I can't remember what else he said about the great one. Ralph Kiner, he declared another time, digressing to baseball, would have been the greatest power hitter of all time if it hadn't been for his sciatic nerve. Pulling out a book one day, he changed my life with a reading, saying, this doesn't have to do with anything else we've been discussing, I just want you to hear it. And he proceeded to read a long passage from Wittgenstein's *Culture and Value*, a book I still go back to over and over, a book I sometimes read with Diogenes' voice and cadence in my head, a book I still give as a gift to the right reader. And what's important in this, for teachers, I think, is that Diogenes didn't reach for Wittgenstein because it illustrated something we were struggling with. It was something else. It linked indirectly. Whatever we were doing brought the Wittgenstein to his mind. And very briefly it changed the altitude of the discussion. Made us a glimpse something from another angle. Then away. It was overflow; it was fertility. It was what the literary critic James Wood celebrates in novelists as *surplus*. So patient and methodical teaching us one book, Diogenes didn't see what he was doing as a linear progression of understanding. It was the life moving inside him reaching out to the life stumbling in us. And he wasn't sentimental about this in the least. When he gave back our first set of papers, he said, there are two grades in the back: the first is the grade your paper deserves, the second is the one I'll record because I know some of you need grades to go on to other things, and I'm not going to take on the whole system at your expense—*but the first grade is the one you deserve*. I got a C, the only C I ever received in school, a C that was a blow but that also made me smile. It said: you are being read for once, not flattered. It said, you aren't as far along as you might think you are. It said—for Diogenes told this famous anecdote too, from ancient Egypt—there is no royal road to understanding.

Once, after class, a student was offering earnest postmodern critiques to Diogenes. Diogenes waited him out, then said very calmly, you need to read the church fathers. What are they going to tell me? the frustrated student asked. You need to read the church fathers, Diogenes repeated. Why? the student pressed. Diogenes: Let them show you what to seek.

He loved Augustine, I remember now, and more than once quoted the old bishop saying, the food that we dream of is very like the food we eat when we're awake, except that, what? It doesn't *nourish* us. How insistent Diogenes was that we think of truth, wisdom, knowledge not as something that satisfied some objective, external criteria but as something instead that nourishes us. How bracing it was to hear someone steeped in philosophy defend the realm of felt experience. Even when his ideas weren't convincing, the fact that everything he said was completely internalized, completely believed was thrilling. On the New Testament miracles, on the Virgin Birth, on the Resurrection: I believe them (the apostles) on other things, Diogenes said, shrugging; why shouldn't I believe them on those? He taught me to love the incident in the New Testament in which a man healed by Jesus is rebuked for violating the Sabbath by carrying his mat. The New Testament records the man's response: The one who made me well told me to do it. Diogenes added: I do whatever That Man says.

He was cantankerous, crusty, charismatic, impatient, eccentric, a little cheerless, sometimes harsh (he and I collided over Kant—he rebuked me hard and publicly), and yet I loved him, and I love these memories of him and hold him up as an example of an artist-teacher at the peak of his power. He was fully inside something, he fully inhabited a vision of the world, and his passion for what he believed made his mind roam freely. Woolf again on Shakespeare: his plays were the perfectly elastic envelope of his thought. Like Diogenes' lectures. I'm a little giddy just recalling the experience, and deeply grateful for that first-year class.

And yet. Here's the other side of his charisma: people got lost in Diogenes' class. Most of us didn't have philosophy backgrounds. This was a roomful of seminary students headed in all kinds of directions. Diogenes opened up his very fertile mind for us. He was serenely electric in the classroom. People went on talking about his arguments and discussions outside of class and long after the course was over. He woke us up to something big and provocative and valuable. Every inch the Emersonian guide, and so much of what I celebrate when I think about great teaching. And yet, people were lost, and a T.A. named Bill rescued a great number of us by organizing study sessions before the exam to make sure people could connect the dots and face the final. Of that final exam, Diogenes told us his strategy: I might just say, here's some stuff, what the hell do you make of that? As of course he would. But it left Bill to fill white boards with all the topics we'd covered, and over the course of many hours he went back through every one, very practically, and answered everyone's questions. This is important to see. To understand what we were learning, we needed more than Diogenes.

I benefited enormously from Bill's review sessions, escaped with an A that was probably, in truth, a Diogenes B-. But Diogenes, not Bill, was a fork in the road for me. I needed to think about religion differently, and I didn't have a grammar or vocabulary to do so. Diogenes did. I hung on his words. And even if I never became a true believer in his approach, it was exactly what I needed at the time, and when I think about great teaching I have to sit back down in that Romanesque room once again in my mind. Because I want every student to have experiences like that, multiple times, in a whole range of disciplines. Leibniz was a *hell* of a lot smarter than the Apostle Paul. What a thrilling thing to say, especially since he followed up, almost as an aside, with this: but Paul is the greater figure. And I suppose I want more teachers like Diogenes because that kind of fullness is too rare. It's okay to me that Bill had to stand there holding the ladder while we young minds tried to climb. Great teachers aren't all great in the same way. All of them are incomplete, their own kind of work in progress. That's why we try to have lots of them. No one teacher is everything any one student needs. Diogenes wasn't everything I needed. But he summoned us up to something large and worthy and inspired. And, my God, the views were glorious.

ON BEING CHARMED

What love and happy pride of love inspires these words! So charming, and there is nothing more heartfelt than this scene in all the rest of this charming story.

— Tolstoy, on a piece written by one of his students

For me, the prestige and glory of the teaching profession is forever secured by the simple fact that for several years and with tremendous gusto Leo Tolstoy ran a school. If we can't learn something about teaching life from the author of *Anna Karenina*, we should switch the lights off now in all our classrooms, let students live online.

Years before he wrote *Anna Karenina* and *War and Peace*, Tolstoy organized a school for the children of peasants on his estate, and, as one would expect, he taught them how to write. Most remarkable to me in reading Tolstoy's accounts of his students is the wonder and delight he experiences in their emerging wonder and delight. Two boys, struggling to recompose a story, for example, stay behind to work from seven o'clock to eleven o'clock at night, and they get mad when Tolstoy wants them to stop. After one of those boys has a breakthrough, Tolstoy, the witness, is moved and even overwhelmed by what Emerson would no doubt have called a kind of awakening: "I cannot convey the feeling of agitation, joy, fear and almost regret that I experienced in the course of that evening," Tolstoy writes. "I felt from this day a new world of pleasure and suffering had opened for him—the world of art. It seemed to me that I had seen what nobody ever has the right to see—the conception of the mysterious flower of poetry." He goes on: "It was terrible and joyful for me."

When another student writes a story and misuses a word, Tolstoy pauses to delight in that too. The student had used the word "hastened" without an object. The grammar teacher, Tolstoy notes, feels the need to correct this, but for him the clipped use "lights up the whole picture" of the story: "'Hastened' requires a complement—'hastened to do what?' the teacher has to ask. It is simply said, 'Mother took the money and hastened, carried it away to bury…' and this is charming."

For me, it is the observation of Tolstoy's that is charming. I once worked with a team of teachers in a writing program at a school in New York. I offered that anecdote to my colleagues ever year to remind us all to be alive and available to being charmed by student work. Nothing pleases me more as a teacher than when a colleague flags me down, or seeks me out and says, you have to read this, you have to see what Jamie wrote, or Ella. Sincere delight like that is part of instructional success. If, in writing, students are building a relationship with language and with their own inner world, if they are learning "the beauty of expressing life in words," the teacher needs to build a relationship to the students' discovery, to their frustrations and delight, to their relationship with language—not to their deficits and proficiencies. The first step in getting this orientation right seems to me a simple capacity to be moved and charmed by voice and self-discovery. If Tolstoy's example is apt, any teacher who doesn't experience fairly regular moments of joy and delight in student work is either in the wrong business or else is designing the work poorly.

I suppose we don't attend to this part of the job enough because we're anxious to make clear to everyone that our students are improving. We're stressed to make sure we see and show growth. When I've talked about being charmed as a category to value, I've been challenged by both parents and teachers: how does that help students get better? And it's not that I don't want to see improvement too, but that I want to see the right thing celebrated, which is discovery, which is transformation, which is understanding opening up for someone. When we talk about growth, we sometimes sound interested in a frame-by-frame progression of skills rather than the real-life motion of the young mind, which doesn't switch on all its lights at once, or in the same order from kid to kid. I want to ban all phrases from teacher talk that begin with caution: "We have to be careful to...." "We have to make sure we're not...." In his comments on his students, Tolstoy is not playing defense. In fact, he warns us not to be like "bad sculptors" with our students, over-adding to one side, or over-chiseling, then compensating with over-balancing the other. On my New York team, we used to say, this isn't deficit repair. We're looking for what's moving, and we're working with that movement.

I suppose what I'm describing is simply an authentic response to a piece of work, a relaxed response, full of the freedom Virginia Woolf urged. Unless we avoid the state of mind that is always looking for what to correct, students will experience their school life as a long line of skill acquisition. Learning becomes a process of fixing and adding things. There's no time for charm on an assembly line.

Being charmed isn't the only right response of a teacher to student work. I'll acknowledge again that this isn't a book about pedagogy or strategy but about mindset and a teacher's positioning, a teacher's relationship to their work. There are other oars that need to be pulled; other books pull them. But if a teacher never describes herself as being charmed by her students, or some equivalent, I'm suspicious of whatever else the teacher offers by way of feedback. On the writing team I worked on, we made it a point to have students read work aloud at the beginning of each class, and we noted and named what worked in those pieces and what we loved. Then the team crafted mini-lessons of next moves for the group, and we targeted specific challenges for individual students to try. But we began with what we loved. I believe the order matters.

I still remember a student piece that one of my colleagues, Erin, shared with the team. Her sixth-grader had writer's block. He was complaining about writing at the end of a long week. He doodled in the margins of the page. But he wrote. His final line was "I tried to write." Here was Erin's comment at the end of an entry that struggled. I like to think it would have pleased Tolstoy. "And write you did! Really, I don't know if you see what I see, but from my view, I see a bright young man who sometimes has the unfortunate luck of having a writing class during the last period of the day on a FRIDAY at the end of a long week, and yet he puts his pen to the page, and he writes! And each day he writes a little more, and a little more, and the questions he has are making him curious and making him struggle, and growing his brain. And it is beautiful to watch." The next time the student had that class, he wrote about that same struggle, but he did it from the teacher's perspective. That was beautiful to watch too.

I had a student once, again in seventh grade in North Carolina, who struggled mightily with controlling his attention. The good thing was, he distracted himself more than he distracted the class, and he was big-hearted, and his parents were supportive, so we were all in a good place for the year. And yet, the student did crazy things. The team of us decided to let him have a stress ball in class to occupy his fidgety hands. Once, when students were working independently, he came up to me and said, yeah, uh, Mr. Shy, my ball is in the light fixture back there. He pointed to his table, the tray of fluorescent lights above. I thought I saw it.

How did it get there? I asked. I don't know, he said, and he tried to register genuine astonishment, as if he had looked away for one moment and the laws of nature breached. I smiled. Did it just leap up there when you weren't paying attention? I asked. I don't know, he said. He tried to sustain his disbelief. I smiled again, and he knew two things in that moment: he knew I knew he wasn't telling me the truth, but he also knew he wasn't in trouble. Now he smiled too. Let's rescue this truant ball, I said, and we went back to his seat, climbed up on the table, and fished the ball free. Another time, my colleague was walking around his class, and this same student was playing a video game. If I remember the account right, it was golf. My colleague stood behind him. The student didn't know he was there. Other students saw him, though. The student kept playing the game, and the class watched to see what my colleague would do. He did nothing. Finally, when he realized there was a teacher behind him, the student pulled his hands back from the keyboard like he'd touched a red-hot stove. He feigned disbelief again, this time at what had taken over his screen. My colleague asked what he was doing, and he said he didn't know what happened. My colleague suggested they contact Microsoft or Dell to run a check on his computer. Then the student smiled, and he got back on task, and my colleague left him alone, but then, after class, he told me, he kept him back and spoke with him one-on-one. We reset, he said, laughing. We rebooted. And I called his parents to let them know what had happened, so we could keep an eye on him together.

All of us on that team were charmed by this student, I have to say, because his mischief had no malice, and when he was lost he wasn't trying to get away with something so much as he was trying, often very unsuccessfully, to manage his own divided mind. School as we have structured it was not a natural fit for him. The wind was in his face not at his back. I liked that he could still smile at his own struggles and connect to adults regardless. My own progress with that student wasn't so much moment-by-moment breakthrough as a long, slow commitment to sticking with him while he worked—and got expert help—and letting some levity into the failures or struggles so that we had a relationship for the hard work ahead. Years later, students would come up to me sometimes and ask if I was aware that my colleague had stood behind this 7th grader while he played video golf unaware. Oh, I was well aware, I told them. We do talk, you know. He just stood there, they'd say. Then they would smile and shake their heads. They liked the incident—that it happened, how it unfolded, how softly it resolved. Honestly, I'm not sure why students remembered it so fondly, but they did. My colleague did too. It somehow was for that class a moment of joy. In its small way, maybe, it's what Tolstoy felt, being charmed.

I was on the receiving end of this Tolstoyan virtue as well, when I was no poster child of charm. The teacher my mother says changed my life was a fourth-grade reading teacher, Ms. Abel. Apparently, I was a handful as a ten-year-old. I think it's fair to say I was a know-it-all. My father was an intellectual wolf in businessman sheep's clothing, and I inherited something of both his restlessness and his ferocious pursuit of clarity through books. Even as a kid, I argued, like my father, in order to win arguments. (I am still learning how hollow those victories usually are.) Kids like me can irritate and threaten teachers. I was one myself, and I've taught many of them since. We interrupt with too many questions designed not to clarify what the class needs to know but to prove our own smarts to the teacher and the world. We quote books none of the other kids have read—because they haven't read them. In group work, we are competitive with classmates where we might be kind, hoping other people's failures magnify our own proud successes. It takes a teacher with a lot of heart to even want to help a kid like that. Apparently, Ms. Abel did exactly that for me. He's reading off the charts, she said to my mother, but he's got to learn how to be with other people. Let me work on that this year.

Which she proceeded to do. And she did it not by correcting me all the time, or pointing out my many flaws, but by giving me interesting things to do, by inviting my curiosity, by paying attention, by watching my interactions with other kids more than my standardized scores, and, mostly, by being charmed by things I did. She laughed at me when I was showing off when she might have rebuked or reined me in. She never took me in the hall to point out my arrogance; she pulled me away and gave me something different to do. She won me through indirection, and I trusted her because my quirks made her laugh, and my arrogance didn't threaten her.

One day two friends and I were moving a piano down the hall. I don't remember why. We'd finished our work. Ms. Abel suggested a way we could be of use. We were pushing a piano down the hall. She came out to check on us. We hushed her. We whispered that she needed to be quiet. We were stealing a piano. She laughed and let us go, charmed by our passing silliness. What did that do? Why do I remember it? We arguers go through the world competing. But Ms. Abel turned my shoulders just a little. Her receiving of who I was without judgment or threat took character, security, toughness, but mostly love. The feeling I have recalling her is what she gave to me. And she showed me a different way to walk and be and encounter, and when I was ridiculous, she laughed, and when I understood difficult texts, she praised, and then thought of other things I might try next. What an extraordinary gift a teacher like that is. What skill she had to pull that off. What grace.

THE HARDEST MONTH
I EVER TAUGHT

The Saharas must be crossed as well as the Nile.
— Emerson

Sixteen years into my teaching career, I moved to New York City to help launch an ambitious global school, and in this start-up environment I felt like a rookie all over again. The whole building was a hive of start-up excitement, and it took a while to really settle in. We occupied a ten-story warehouse in the art-gallery district of Manhattan. The final furniture and equipment were still being installed the weekend before students arrived. I remember showing up early that first morning and finding the night crew sweeping away plaster dust in the stairwells with push brooms, the final work complete right before students arrived.

Then we launched into the work we'd prepared to do. I was teaching sixth and seventh grade history on teams with English teachers. The sixth graders were energetic and eager to learn. We were studying the ancient world, and my colleague and I decided to have students make a cave in our room and decorate the inside with imitations of ancient cave art and then decorate the outside with what the class decided was our modern equivalent: graffiti. We had it up and running in time to hand parents flashlights for their Curriculum Night tour. The sixth-grade students seemed locked-in and engaged; the teachers did too. We had a great start.

Seventh grade was another story, though. There were thirty-six seventh-graders in all, divided into two sections. Both sections were boy heavy. Unlike the sixth graders, their energy was really difficult to focus. My English-teacher colleague Sharan and I had prepared a first unit we were excited about—but the kids weren't excited about it. I was teaching the Silk Road. From the very first day, that caravan stalled, and I couldn't figure out what I was doing wrong. Students talked when they were supposed to be listening; they weren't doing their work; they were disruptive and disrespectful and cynical about assignments. And they weren't happy. I was teaching these students the exact same way I taught students in North Carolina, but I wasn't effective in the least. I kept students back after class, trying to steer and motivate them. I had to implement the kind of I-need-your-attention signals that always drove me crazy and that I sometimes thought I had too much dynamism and authority to need. I needed them now: a hand in the air, a "clap once if you can hear me," whatever it took. If I was teaching them something directly, I had to tell them over and over to write things down. I could be up front giving directions, and students would stare back passively unless I said, write this down. By which I meant type. Cutting edge laptops were not our friends in those early days. I was forever asking students to close their laptops so we could focus on something together. When laptops were open, I was forever watching screens for games. If students were discussing something in groups, they did whatever they could to make the class break out in laughter. Not every student, of course, but a critical mass of them. Over and over I had to review protocols for everything from where to put your backpack to how to enter and exit the room. We didn't have bells. I had to remind them that I would dismiss classes, not their own judgment that it was time to get up and leave. They challenged my feedback. If I gave back papers, someone would say out loud, I can't understand what you wrote here. Another would say, also out loud, I can't read your handwriting. A vocal group said they didn't like what we were studying. They said it was dumb. They said they'd learned about it already. They said the readings were too hard, too boring. They asked when we could do something fun. Once when I tried to make a whimsical connection to the Vikings by showing a Capital One commercial, the first student to respond said, I don't know what this has to do with what we're supposed to be learning.

Obviously, we teachers were being tested by kids who may or may not have wanted to be there. Sharan wondered if, for a bunch of them, it was their parents' idea to try this new school. Maybe they wanted to be elsewhere. The unspoken deal seemed to be that we had to earn the right for them be interested in whatever we thought we were there to do. They weren't brazen so much as cynical. And then sometimes some were brazen. I knew that ultimately it was on us, it was our job to meet these students where they were, but we just couldn't figure out how to. In my seventeenth year of teaching, I felt as helpless as I'd ever felt. That class, divided into two sections, was full of alpha males who kept up a running competition to control the dynamic of the room and stir the most laughter. I raised my voice in that first month in ways I never had in North Carolina. Every day was exhausting, and everything I've been describing in this book about great teaching was essentially absent from my room. The Silk Road was more like the Dead Sea, and we were more *Breakfast Club* study hall than a scene from *The Dead Poets Society*.

Sharan was also exasperated. Later, she told me she'd pondered quitting. It was clear we'd underestimated two major things: the extraordinary logistics of a large-scale start-up school, and the challenge of building a culture without traditions and a past. We were building the airplane, our running joke went, as we were flying it. We had had workshops on every aspect of school life from curriculum design to advisory and classroom norms, but we had no inherited community life, no muscle memory for how we were together, and in the very early days it felt like floors of talented faculty improvising community as best we could. The irony was that a lot of the kids our school attracted in that first year—certainly the seventh graders—needed stability over creativity and order over freedom. Sharan and I had designed for creativity and freedom. When the kids wouldn't go where we wanted them to go, I got frustrated and helpless, and was not, for that month, a very good teacher.

I remember walking around my neighborhood one night after work talking on the phone with a colleague in North Carolina who had been a kind of mentor. I don't know what to do, I told her. It's like they need old-school structures. But if we go too hard that way, I'm afraid we'll lose them—and give up on everything we're trying to do. Yep, you'll lose them, my colleague said matter-of-factly. I agree, I said, so I'm thinking of going the other way completely. What will that look like? she asked. I don't know yet, I said. You could lose them that way too, she said.

One day several weeks in, as part of a discussion of something else, one of the students talked about their previous school. He'd been bullied there. I saw some other boys nodding. Did you go there too? I asked. They did. And it didn't become a big therapeutic moment, but I let them talk for a while about their experiences before they came to our school. Some of the girls talked about being made fun of or ostracized where they had been as well. And the thing was, they were listening to each other now, not interrupting, not goofing off. So I let them talk on. I think all I said that day was, that sounds really hard. And probably I added, we want this place to be different. And the conversation itself was like a valve releasing pressure. It didn't revolutionize our classroom community, but *something* released. It was a seam I thought we might be able to widen. It led me to invite the other section to talk about their previous schools as well. I went to Sharan afterward and said, everything we prepared was elegant—and wrong. Let's stop and try something else.

Honestly, I don't think it would have mattered much *what* we decided to teach them next. We just needed to shift gears. It needed to feel different. And whatever it was needed to feel like a re-set without a giving in. Sharan and I went to our middle school director and told him what was going on. He had seen and approved of the initial curriculum, and now we said we needed to suspend it for a while, maybe three weeks, maybe four. Would he support that? This is where being in start-up mode helped. He did.

What we ended up designing was a unit on "The Examined Life." Essentially, I taught them a very targeted introduction to thinking philosophically—about the world but also themselves. To leverage their clear attention shift when they talked about their past schools, Sharan developed a unit on personal writing. We pulled back on homework. I always began class with a quotation on the board, and first they'd write a response in their notebooks, and then we'd talk about it. That initial writing was as much an exercise in quieting and slowing them down as getting them to think hard. They got used to looking for the quote when they came in. And I went for broke with these choices. I tried to raise the altitude of class work even as we slowed it down. I tried to flatter their aspirations. We used excerpts from Socrates, quotes from Wittgenstein, Zadie Smith, David Foster Wallace. We read short texts about the costs and benefits of technology. Was Google making us stupid? an *Atlantic* article asked. We debated that. I used anything I could think of to get them thinking about themselves and the world around them and what it required from us as students, and as people. Meanwhile, in English, they wrote about their lives. We asked them to write about whether it was harder being their age or their parents' age. We had them write about school itself.

Sharan had them write six-word memoirs and poems. Writing first thing every day, we got a little bit quieter, calmer. Writing about big ideas that have been kicked around for over two thousand years, we got a little more serious too. We told them we were doing this unit without telling them at first we were abandoning what we'd planned. At the end of the four weeks, we asked for a very brief reflection paper. No material was tested. Then we gathered students into one room to talk about what we'd done, asked if they had ideas about why we had done it, and asked for their feedback. I still remember that Sharan and I noticed a small but significant change in our collective world, a settling, but when we asked the students if they had observed a shift, their response was, no, not really. Some things did sink in. Some of them liked philosophy quotes. Others didn't. They were in seventh grade. Houdini couldn't have outwitted their hormones and their interests and biographies—and New York teeming, the city sirens wailing right outside our windows, on crowded 10th Avenue. Having made this brief detour, we shifted gears again and rejoined the Silk Road, as originally planned. Sharan went back to her English units. The year went on.

And it was different just enough now, and we did better as a class. I kept putting quotations or provocative questions on the board some days to start. That may have been the best single tactic for this unsettled group: some quiet writing at the beginning of each class. More than once I wondered why The Examined Life had to be the outlier, the lifeboat, rather than the substance of the class itself, the ship. Bukhara, Samarkand, the Buddhist caves at Dunhuang, caravan stops, deserts and seas, Marco Polo, Ibn Battuta, Chinese porcelain blue as the new-moon sky, all of this was interesting to me, but was that really more important for these kids than thinking about meaning and dilemmas and how we negotiate contradiction and complexity and unknowns and cities—and bullies? We did what we could. Sharan and I talked about that experience for years. I wasn't sure we would ever break through with that group. Many of them seemed that cynical. And we weren't sure we would make it to the end with anything like our sanity, much less our joy, intact.

But slowly, without drama, we improved, all of us, and, in retrospect, I see that it wasn't The Examined Life itself that did it. We had no traction or tradition yet at our school. We were building that plane as we were flying it. It took time, but something like community began to form in the thousand unheralded ways it does. My colleagues and I went to see our students sing in their concerts or play basketball or soccer. We organized what the kids called the greatest field trip ever, following Silk Road cultures via subway, through neighborhoods of Queens. We had blunt one-on-one conversations pretty regularly with some of the boys who went on struggling in class. After one particularly bright kid handed in a dazzling paper, we called him out to the hall one day and, holding out his work, said, the person who wrote this is far too talented to be squandering his attention and energy in class the way he has been. Tell him to take advantage, we said, handing back the paper; and tell him to keep writing like this because it's extraordinary and can't really be taught.

Once, I saw the group of alpha males gathered around a table. They were piling toward the center. A math teacher and I went over to see if it was something that needed to be broken up. They were arm wrestling. They looked up as if they were in trouble. The math teacher set his bag down. Who's the strongest one here? he said. Who's been winning? They relaxed. Then they laughed and hooted as he pushed up his sleeve to arm-wrestle their champ.

Sometime that year, we read excerpts from *Don Quixote*, and one of the boys who would not take anything seriously, including, I think, for a while, himself, woke up to those stories, and when other people criticized the silliness of the Don, he defended his crazy heroism, and that defense by this indifferent student was one of the greatest triumphs of the year.

When it came time to read Shakespeare, Sharan and I trimmed *Henry IV, Part I* and had students read it, then memorize a passage each, then perform it at a final exhibition for parents. And who knows if the consolations of that coming-of-age play seeped into their young minds at all that difficult year—a young prince living wild and reckless, but waiting on, and sure of the transformation to come. We made it through. We made it. In the coming years, that group went on having some struggles as a class. Some of them made some really bad choices. At different times, they divided into cliques. One time, when one of the boys got into a stupid fight with one of his friends and was sitting outside the office while the administration decided whether he would be suspended or expelled, I went over and sat next to him, just sat there for a while, because he was too scared of what might happen, this alpha male, to speak. We shared a tough silence I'll never forget. All the way through high school, whenever we saw any of those kids in the halls, we greeted them by name and asked what was going on. We loved catching up with them. We had a fondness for the class. Most of them were going to be just fine, I would think, most of the time. Now as I write this, many are doing really interesting things in impressive places. And it's not that what we did in seventh grade set them up to be fine, but it set up the relationships we went on having with them through school, the passing conversations, the shared recollections, and those seemed to matter both to them and to us.

For a long time, some of the students liked to remind me of the time I tried to read from *Winnie-the-Pooh* in class, and one of the boys couldn't control his laughter—for this is where they were at the time—whenever I read aloud the childhood word for excrement: pooh. Some of them liked to remind me how we squeezed in a week's worth of activity into a two-day trip to Washington, and how the rooms

52

weren't ready in the hotel and we were all camped out in the lobby with our bags, and how two of our boys started a small fire in their microwave that genuinely wasn't their fault, and how we saw their drama teacher perform the lead role in *Richard III* at the Folger, and he, as Richard, pacing the stage eating strawberries, came over to the front row and handed my colleague a strawberry while the play went on. On the bus the next morning, as we rode to Ford's Theater, I took the driver's microphone and narrated random facts about Lincoln that I'm pretty sure no one was listening to.

To cap it all off, I was yelled at by the Capitol Police for allowing the kids to jaywalk. Remember that, Mr. Shy? Students would ask me this later. I remember that it was Ms. Reedy's fault, I tell them, smiling, and that I took the fall for her, is what I remember. They laugh. Real good, the cop yelled at me. Real good role modeling there. I offered no defense. Reedy up ahead, looking back, shrugged an apology, laughing too.

AGAINST ENDLESS PREPARATION

The value of these is conceived as lying largely in the remote future; the child must do these things for the sake of something else he is to do; they are mere preparations.

— John Dewey, "My Pedagogic Creed"

The voice and looming mustachioed presence of my sixth-grade teacher Mr. Wiseman still haunts me. I don't think he was happy in his job. He'd been selling insurance in a neighboring town before making the transition to school. From this long distance—over forty years now—I'd say he didn't know what he wanted. He was tall and taciturn. I don't remember him smiling or laughing ever. His life lessons were warnings rather than hopeful advice. Once we made a series of models: model rooms, model cars, model buildings. I was lousy with my hands, and he let me know my work was sub-par, told me I had one more chance to make the grade on the last model. I think because my father was a confident, charismatic figure, I wasn't easily intimidated by strong men. I think Mr. Wiseman knew that. There was a little bit of rivalry and power play in his demeanor and in our interactions. When he walked around the room, he shook chalk in his hand like a gambler about to throw unlucky dice. He wanted me to know very clearly who was boss. And that's what I remember about him, and that's pretty much all except for a catch phrase he had, a rebuke he issued to the boys in the room whenever we irritated him. We were in sixth grade; junior high in those days started in seventh. The following year we were going to leave our suburban elementary school to go to the town's one junior high, and Mr. Wiseman wanted us to know we weren't even close to being ready. "You walk around junior high with that chip on your shoulder," he used to announce whenever one of us did something, "someone will knock—it—off." So many chips on his own shoulder, I see now, were asking for that favor.

Mr. Wiseman wasn't the only sixth-grade teacher who repeated to us the importance of getting ready for junior high. And, of course, our teachers genuinely wanted us to succeed, I know that, but they also wanted to be seen, I think, as having done *their* job well. Too much of a teacher's mind can be dogged by this pressure to think about the next thing students will be doing, rather than being immersed in what we're doing now, in front of us, for the irretrievable year that we will have these particular students. I've known eighth-grade teachers who target certain skills because they say students will need them in high school. I remember English department meetings about five-paragraph essays being the skill a student needed to take with them to ninth grade. *That* was why we needed to teach it well. Too many schools cling to programs and curricula because they're sure they're necessary to equip students to handle college. The higher you go up the grades, the more likely it is that teachers will see their job as preparing students for more advanced work in their own discipline. The history teacher teaches students to be young historians, the science teacher young chemists, etc. They seem to be preparing the whole room for that work, even if, in reality, maybe one student in twenty—maybe—will go on to do deeper work in their field. The rest of them need—what exactly, in that year in which you teach them 180 or so times? Skills for standardized tests? A taste of every discipline to see which one will stick? And if students have seven classes, say, every day, is the optimal experience of school for them really seven daily preparations for the next level of work in seven disciplines?

Some of this is pedagogy. Most of this is mindset. The main aim of elementary school shouldn't be preparation for middle school. The main aim of middle school shouldn't be preparation for high school. The main aim of high school shouldn't be preparation for college. The main aim of college is not preparation for a first job. Just as the point of falling in love young isn't to get ourselves ready for the real thing later (though it helps), or the point of reading *Harry Potter* isn't to make sure we're ready to read *The Catcher in the Rye* or *Beloved* (though, please do). Legendary Deerfield Academy headmaster Frank Boyden resisted the urge to have his students practice the freedom of university life, which some rival schools emphasized: "there is no point in going to college before you get there," he declared. We should ban from the teacher's lounge any claim that students need to power through something simply in order to get themselves ready for the next thing. It makes them the object of our program rather than the subject of their own learning—and life. It makes them the object of our program rather than the subject of their own learning—and life.".

The larger problem is not bad faith but lack of vision for what school and teaching are for. This—and his own unhappiness—was the reason I think Mr. Wiseman struggled. The mean that teachers regress to over and over is something like this: We're here to give students skills so they can use them in their next set of work. We're going to teach them how to write an essay because they need to write essays to get into college. We're going to teach them how to do this math to get them ready for the SAT. In this model, students show up in our class with half-empty toolboxes. Our job is to place the hammer of historian work or the cylinders of a chemist's craft in their kit, then send them on. To switch the metaphor, it's a progressive dinner, academy style. The goal is an overflowing plate of skills. But this approach is just too linear and mechanical. The vision is too small and unimaginative. Kids are much more than consumers of content and developers of skills. This is what Alison Gopnik in her book *The Gardener and the Carpenter* criticized as a parenting model focused on producing a certain kind of kid—like a carpenter—rather than giving them fertile conditions to grow—like a gardener. John Stuart Mill made a similar claim in a broader context: "Human nature is not a machine to be built after a model, and set to do exactly the work prescribed for it, but a tree, which requires to grow."

Mill wrote from experience. His father famously made the education of his son an experiment—beginning with learning Greek at age three—that turned Mill into a kind of genius but that also eventually broke him. He had become a "well-equipped ship with a rudder," Mill wrote in his autobiography, "but no sail." John Dewey would have sympathized: "I believe that education which does not occur through forms of life, forms that are worth living for their own sake, is always a poor substitute for the genuine reality and tends to cramp and to deaden." That "for their own sake" is the key to a great classroom, one in which students do things that have value in and of themselves, not because they're a dry run for the real stuff to come.

The main problem with endless preparation is that it dams the flowing life of learning and sees education as acquisition instead. Schools look like factories putting iPhones together more than the spaces where iPhones get conceived. But a secondary problem with endless preparation is that we don't, in fact, know what we're preparing kids for. Not anymore. Not really. Or rather, we know we're preparing them for a world we can't see or predict. All conversations about twenty-first century learning eventually come around to the unpredictability of a rapidly changing world. To take one example, the XQ Super School Project, a non-profit that encourages and funds educational innovation, wants to cultivate "Original Thinkers for an Uncertain World: Sense-makers and generative thinkers, creating many ideas in ambiguous and new situations." That impulse seems exactly right—and not entirely new. Humility in the face of the future (and the past) made sense to John Dewey over a hundred years before: "With the advent of democracy and modern industrial conditions, it is impossible to foretell definitely just what civilization will be twenty years from now. Hence it is impossible to prepare the child for any precise set of conditions. To prepare him for the future life means to give him command of himself; it means so to train him that he will have the full and ready use of all his capacities." Dewey made that claim in 1897.

Dip into recent literature on creativity and creative industries, and you will hear little else. In his book *Creativity, Inc.*, Pixar co-founder Ed Catmull tells stories of his company's determination to not just duplicate past successes but to keep conceiving the next and the new, asking, "how do we go about creating the unmade future?" You don't have to be in the animation game to know we're all somehow in this boat. At my New York school, we brought in a speaker one time who works in the field of environmental law. A student asked him how he got into that specialized area. His response? The field didn't exist when he graduated law school. He couldn't have prepared himself to go into environmental law because it wasn't around to prepare for. And it's not just careers; all of life is movement toward the unknown. We need imagination and courage to face it. Schools should major in those virtues and cultivate the nimbleness that lets you enter uncertainty with confidence, grace, and skill.

Kids do need clear narratives about what they're learning, and we need a plan for their larger progression, yes, but that plan and that learning should feel like the rest of our experience of the world: dynamic, complex, calibrated differently for different people, connected to all kinds of interesting—and challenging—things, and viewed over and over through changing lenses. Life is not one long static chain we build a link at a time. Learning should be as varied and changeable as life. Again, I'm not advocating a Romantic free-for-all. My humanities colleagues and I used to hold ourselves to two standards: have joy in the classroom, and have purpose and narrative. Organizing learning for that sense of purpose is not deadening if the purpose itself is worthy of the students. It's just that if we begin with all of the things we have to prepare kids for *next*, we might miss the chance to give them a robust experience now.

The practices that matter in school aren't preparations for other things that are ends in themselves but versions of things that are ends in themselves. You could argue that as long as students are practicing valuable skills and learning important things it doesn't matter if the teacher sees their point as preparation for next-level work. That might be true. But telling the right story about what we're doing in school feels important for student engagement. When we frame all our efforts as getting ready for future efforts, we're planting the seeds for mid-life crises, when you finally look up and wonder what you're readying yourself to do after all.

There are ways, I think, to keep kids engaged in their present, even as we try to develop their strength for later work too. We learn to write, for example, not primarily because colleges require essays that we're practicing for but because writing facilitates discovery and expression and voice. It extends our thinking and our sense of the world. Discovery and expression and voice and extended understanding are components of a rich life regardless of the stage you're in. In writing, students practice an important dimension of life and learn ways to do that better. Of course, writing is also a practical, useful skill. Great. Indeed. But that should be a collateral benefit, not the sole mission, or the sole reason, for learning how to write. Or, to take another example, group-based project work is sometimes spoken of as a 21st century skill because so much work in the real world anymore is collaborative. And that's good too. If you want to see the importance of collaboration in action, read Ed Catmull's book about Pixar. But the reason for project work in school shouldn't be because it will help you land a job in Silicon Valley. It should be because it engages real student interest and asks kids to plan and work with others to achieve success. We practice collaboration in school because our lives are embedded in communities at all stages. Schools tend to the growth of those capacities in students. They are useful skills, absolutely, but if we don't tell the right story, if we pitch school skills as endless preparations for harder things down the road, we miss opportunities to build intrinsic motivation, real curiosity, lifelong habits of learning, and love of the world and our place in it. We weigh down the joy of learning in the moment.

A lot of this pressure comes from above teachers' heads. I know that. But this is a book about teachers and classrooms and how to best incite life in students—in the midst of conditions sometimes out of the teacher's hands. And it's tragic that those larger conditions discourage talented, passionate people from even thinking about the teaching life. And whenever the structures of school make it feel like an assembly line of preparation for students and teachers, it's unforgivable. In the meantime, for those who step into a classroom despite the headaches and the rain forest of red tape, what we *can* do is preserve the right mindset at all costs—thinking rightly about the job, and remembering that people go on reporting being changed by their encounters with great teachers, regardless, or in spite of the politics and policies.

Here, I think it's worth reminding ourselves—we adults—that we are mid-growth just like our students. Our future is still unpredictable too. None of us teaches, or lives, from a vantage of completed understanding. We don't look back from where we've arrived and see exactly how things really are and so how they should be ordered and taught. We're not coaching through megaphones from the finish line. I'm afraid this is what Mr. Wiseman was doing, alas. We teachers are mid-growth ourselves. Our own understanding is partial and unfinished. Veterans of false starts and changed opinions, we should teach as fellow travelers hitchhiking a little farther down the road. What if we let students know that the real work we're doing together is learning how to manage lifelong growth and change and possibility? What if we said, we're not exactly sure what you'll need to know and do for the life you'll end up living, so we're going to teach you how to stay on the move, intellectually, academically, emotionally, socially? We'll teach you how to be nimble and savvy, world-wise, as well as competent in some skills that go on seeming indispensable to us. And even then we might be wrong.

The literary critic Harold Bloom summarized the seismic shift of Montaigne's essays as treating human life not in terms of being but of becoming. We are always in flux, Montaigne points out, and this qualifies everything. He goes on: "He who remembers having been mistaken so many, many times in his own judgment, is he not a fool if he does not distrust it forever after?" And so, if I approach teaching differently now that I did ten years ago, why on earth would I think I've finally arrived and won't view things differently in ten more? Which is another way of saying that I write with full conviction here, and passion, I hope, because I believe in this work and in teachers and kids, and in what schools can be, but I also know that, as another philosopher said, we see from our own height—not from the peak of Sinai or Olympus.

ON ARTISTS, ENGINEERS, AND DATA DETECTIVES

What is heartbreaking is that increasingly, the process of education, which has the capacity to bring about the formation of the self ... has itself veered toward templated achievement over open-ended process.

— Amy Whitaker, *Art Thinking*

Psychology is a science, and teaching is an art; and sciences never generate arts directly out of themselves. An intermediary inventive mind must make the application, by using its own originality.

— William James, *Talks to Teachers*

We are really shifting the role of an educator to someone who is more of a data-enabled detective.

— Max Ventilla, founder of AltSchool

Watching a great teacher at work can feel like watching a magic show.

— Dana Goldstein, *The Teacher Wars*

Most conversations I've had over the years about teaching loosely describe the job in one of two ways: teachers are artists, or teachers are engineers. These categories aren't about what subject you teach but how you conceive of the job. And it doesn't seem helpful to me to announce that teachers should be both artists and engineers or that schools should be both and that everybody should embody all the best practices known to everyone all the time. Great schools aren't the byproduct of having best practices overlap; they're the product of a compelling vision insisted on. Choices have to be made. The accent has to fall somewhere. A melody needs to organize the well-meaning notes. If this is true for program and curricula, it's also true for teachers themselves. It matters a great deal how the teachers in the building conceive of their work. It matters enormously how they view themselves and what they're there for.

My bias is clearly toward teaching as art, as inspiration, but before I make that case, I'll submit to the right corrective checks and pay my dues to other perspectives. I go on learning as much from the science end of the spectrum, from the systems builders, as I do from more like-minded poets. In my own teaching, I seek them out. I need the balancing talents of teachers who take care of things their art-minded colleagues ignore. *I* need them. Teaching as science is good at asking for evidence of student learning—results that transcend the teacher's judgment. Teaching as science wants to know how we know we're being successful, wants structures to ensure that we see it. The science side of teaching produces rubrics, checklists, strategies, standards, and skill scope and sequences so we can see whether we're getting the results we're hoping for. The science side of teaching satisfies the needs of administrators and policy makers, boards and politicians. To a person on this side of the spectrum, faithfully tending to those accountabilities, artist-teachers draft too many unfinished blueprints, create interesting work for students but don't worry enough about assessing the learning, veer off on quirky tangents that aren't connected to the rest of the students' experience in school, scoff at data too easily, and are just too cavalier about what we can and can't say about learning outcomes, see learning as elusive and mysterious and unpredictable when, in fact, we know a lot of things actually about how students learn, and we need to make informed predictions based on what we know. The science side of teaching is most reassured when citing research, or sometimes, "the research," that well-meaning, conversation-stopping tick of edu-speak, as if one monolithic method steadily shines a light for us to follow— *the research says.* To the science side of things, teaching as art is uncoordinated and ungovernable—a hundred beginnings and too many carefree ends. Intent on inspiring students, the artist-teacher risks being lost when students don't wake up to her incitements. She has no other tricks. And the stakes are too high for each child to allow that kind of gamble. And so, the case seems closed! Let the poets pack their bags.

Alan Bennett's *The History Boys* dramatizes this art-science struggle. In an English school of working-class boys, one of the teachers, Hector, is dynamic, eccentric, Romantic to the core about education—also someone with boundary issues that ultimately get him fired. His classes end with students acting out famous scenes from books and films, and his teaching is full of incident and digression. In the movie version of Bennett's play, the walls of Hector's classroom are covered with a disordered mural of pictures and faces—the kind of peculiar private canon all of us finally assemble.

Hector is the unconcerned, absent-minded teacher who misbuttons his jacket but inspires roomfuls of students because he deeply loves the texts he shares. When he meets with one student after school to discuss a poem by Thomas Hardy, he offers one of the movie's most powerful exchanges because he himself feels the poem so deeply: "The best moments in reading," he says, his eyes squinting closed, "are when you come across something—a thought, a feeling, a way of looking at things—which you had thought special and particular to you. Now here it is, set down by someone else, a person you have never met, someone even who is long dead. And it is as if a hand has come out and taken yours."

Hector's foil, Irwin, is a kind of hired gun whose mission is to get the students into Oxford. He reverse-engineers the process for the students, helps them learn all the tricks of the examination trade, teaches history strategically where Hector teaches like Prometheus sneaking fire from the gods. Punch line and shot across the bow of all artist-Romantics: these working-class students get into Oxford, no doubt thanks to Irwin.

Teachers on Hector's side of the spectrum infuriate teachers who feel responsible for a certain kind of results—like getting students into prestigious universities. Artist-teachers are cool uncles and aunts who just aren't bound to the uninteresting parts of child rearing. They never have to discipline kids or drive them to the doctor or take care of them when they themselves are sick or ground them or put them in time out. With the artist uncle, it's always a highlight reel. It's always good cop. This teacher locates the real work of learning inside the student. They try everything they know to provoke it free, but if the child resists, the artist-teacher finds it easier to step away and say that it can't be manufactured or insisted on. Scientist-teachers, meanwhile, feel more accountable for results, worry over assessments more than their artist counterparts, and know it's their duty to see every kid grow—and measure that growth. They often, too, make the trains run on time. The artist comes up with a great field trip idea; the scientist thinks through all the things that have to be done for the trip to occur at all. Schools would be impossible without these impulses for system and order. Maybe, in the end, I'm arguing for the perfect team, filled with sharp engineers and luminous artists. Maybe each of us should build capacities to move as best we can between both modes.

But for most of this book I want to devote my energy to the other side of the spectrum, to describing the ways that great teaching is an art form, determined to inspire and wake students up, because vitality is the first thing, and, until it fills a school, maybe the only thing that matters. What does it look like? In good anti-engineered fashion, it looks like a lot of things: the teacher in and out of the classroom, talking and presenting with passion and depth, conferencing one-on-one and attending to an individual student's own specific needs, wandering behind the shoulders of small groups while they work, peering at their notebooks or laptops, getting the balance right between letting them wander, letting them struggle, and stepping in with a clarifying question or suggestion, reading student work and deciding the right note of feedback, the right way to push and the right way to praise, talking to students as they come in and when they leave a room, using those bookend moments to quietly repair a relationship with a student you've had to redirect or discipline, using those moments to check on a student you've heard has been stressed for reasons that can't be shared, using those moments to tell a kid in passing that while you haven't yet finished grading the set of class papers, you did read hers, and it made you set your pen down and just read for pleasure and delight it was that good and how did she do that? The teacher in the hall interacting with students, the email he sends home about a kid who's been struggling, the five minutes in a colleague's classroom, talking about the playoffs or the election or the colleague's children, the meeting it's easy to complain about and shut down in and just get through but instead you participate and listen and offer an idea, or volunteer for a task, the music room you just walk into on your way to the library because you hear something lovely coming from inside, and you want to go see what class this is, or if any of them are your students, because they always seem to notice you when you do drop in like this, and you talk about it later—What were you all playing? When will you perform?—and maybe supervising recess you kick a ball around for two minutes in your dress shoes or heels just to show you can let yourself do something your students are better at than you are, and also to make them laugh, and laugh with them, and maybe after school you have duty out front and you wave at parents and speak to one or two, and sometimes you see former students there to pick up a younger sibling and you light up to talk to them and give them the chance to reminisce because as they move up through the grades even adolescent cynicism gets checked by something bigger: an early awareness of the passage of time that is strange and bewildering and haunting, and you're a marker of it for them—and you see them seeing this—and they like that you're still exactly where you were, teaching some new things but some of the same things too (they like to hear)—the black felt back behind the mirror in which they see themselves moving on, more significant than a dozen lesson plans they experienced in your room. To do *that* job well is to inhabit all these modes with fullness, with sincerity, with delight, with attention. I call it art. Education is a science, maybe. Probably. The teaching life is mostly art.

To teach as an artist is to aim for effects that aren't easily scripted. In *The End of Education*, Neil Postman gives ground to educator-engineers but wants to set the limits clearly: "Of course, there are many learnings that are little else but a mechanical skill, and in such cases, there well may be a best way. But to become a different person because of something you have learned—to appropriate an insight, a concept, a vision, so that your world is altered—that is a different matter."

To teach as an artist is also about being a certain kind of person with the kids. The very first time I saw my former colleague Carole teach, her students were doing short scenes from *A Midsummer Night's Dream*. Carole was off to the side, jotting a few notes down, but mostly she was just watching. And what I remember is how readily she laughed at student antics. She was enjoying what they tried. She was a straight shooter who never flattered students falsely. I watched her conference with kids many times, and she ignored the customary formula of offering something positive, then something constructive. There was no spoonful of sugar to help her medicine go down. She read your work and told you what was what, then sent you back to work on it. But she laughed a lot in class, and in those quick syntheses of student work there was never harsh judgment or hint of anything personal. She saw what was going on and gave that insight to students as a gift. So tough, so candid, so unambiguous, so clear. But then so much laughter, so much joy. She was an artist.

In his book *Achieving Our Country*, Richard Rorty sees a similar dichotomy playing out in his own field, philosophy, and in the neighboring discipline of humanities. Rorty defends the category of inspiration at the university level and pushes back on his version of the scientist-instructor, who is intent on what Rorty calls knowingness. Rorty's argument is a gust of wind in the sails of anyone who thinks about teaching as an art form: "When I attribute inspirational value to works of literature," he writes, "I mean that those works make people think there is more to this life than they ever imagined." He goes on: "Inspirational value is not produced by the operations of a method, a science, a discipline, or a profession. It is produced by the individual brush strokes of unprofessional prophets and demiurges. You cannot, for example, find inspirational value in a text at the same time that you are viewing it as the product of a mechanism of cultural production. To view a work in this way gives understanding but not hope, knowledge but not self-transformation."

I love those pairings because both halves are obviously valuable. We need understanding and knowledge, and we need hope and self-transformation. It just so happens that the balance has tilted drastically toward knowledge—and knowingness. Like Rorty, I think the shortage of artistic and inspirational vision is a more pressing issue for schools than an underappreciation of the role of analysis. I look forward to being in a school so filled with teachers inspiring life and imagination and curiosity and hope that we have to call ourselves back to the research and the data. That's exactly the problem I want to have, at least.

Elsewhere, in describing his ideal democratic society, Rorty, a close reader of John Dewey, wrote that it "will not live up to a pre-existent standard, but will be an artistic achievement, produced by the same long and difficult process of trial and error as is required by any other creative effort." Schools should also be artistic achievements, products of collective creativity, filled with beauty for its own sake— performances, assignments, liturgical assemblies—and everywhere life: sincere, relentless, compassionate, joyful life. Artist teachers aren't uncles and aunts, caring only about the fun things. But they are elastic and nimble and responsive to the student life unfolding in front of them—more jazz musician, maybe, than classical conductor—caught up in the music of what's happening, rather than commanding it or steering it only toward the kinds of measurements that make it easiest to think we're doing our job well.

SAGES AND STAGES

When Bacchus is ascendant, when all the world is a pop-
cult blast, then maybe you become a high priest of Apollo,
with his hard graces. Teachers, freelance spirit healers that
they are or ought to be, make a diagnosis, pour out a cure
or two, then see what happens.

— Mark Edmundson, *Why Teach?*

The teachers who made the most difference to me were the
ones who loved their subjects and didn't hide it.

— Jane Tompkins, *A Life in School*

In an early coming-of-age short story, Isaac Babel describes
an afternoon spent by a boy at his grandmother's house by
the Black Sea. The atmosphere of persecution and anti-
Semitism that broods over Babel's early stories sits back here
behind a brief domestic scene crowded with loneliness. At the
end of the story, the grandmother says, chillingly, to the
young narrator, "You must know everything," and then, more
chillingly, "Don't give them your heart."

Every educator like me risks accusations of softness. An
article in my inbox recently warned that research on the soft
skills that have become increasingly popular in schools
(empathy, grit, collaboration) is itself soft. With a nod to
Babel's grandmother, vital teaching doesn't involve all heart

at the expense of hard-won knowledge. So let me interrupt these meditations on Emersonian themes to say that great teachers do sort of know everything—or at least everything they can. They are voracious as well as compassionate, expert as well as agile, and their knowledge reservoir, in fact, spilling over its edges, is one key to their feeling of freedom in the classroom. They are not reaching for things, digging for them; they have knowledge inside; they are drawing on so much, so readily; and all of what they know they adapt with savvy grace to the real students in front of them.

A common criticism of traditional teaching goes like this: Teachers shouldn't be sages on stages. They need to be guides on the side. This understandable Copernican shift moves the attention of education not only from teacher to student but also from teaching to learning. It's very possible to have a certain kind of great teaching going on without a great deal of learning happening. I noted that one of my most memorable teachers, Diogenes Allen, was the Platonic form of a sage but that, without his T.A. to come in behind him, the circle wouldn't have easily closed from teaching to learning. And yet it is teachers who love something else more than their teaching, teachers who love a subject or an author or a category of problems (artificial intelligence, climate change, social justice) who tend to wake students up to what they are going to love or wonder or worry about. You don't even have to love what a particular teacher loves to be engaged. Their ongoing, lifelong passion for whatever they teach—maybe even for anything, or, if you're Babel's grandmother, for everything—is the key. I like Emerson's description of Montaigne's essays: cut them, and they bleed. This kind of fullness of knowledge, a saturation in a field or a world or a subject is the right balance for heart in teaching.

I want to offer some words of defense for the sages, then. Every great teacher is one. But great teachers move off those stages to small groups and to individual students with ease and delight. Still sages, though. For this reason, I want to also defend (as students get older) the humble art form of the at-least occasional lecture. The lecture as lecture gets a bad rap. I've been in faculty meetings where it's a boast to say, we don't lecture anymore; our learning is student-centered; no one lectures. But we should aim our criticism where it belongs: at boring classes, whatever their form. At boringness, not lectures themselves. I agree that inquiry-based learning, student-centered learning is the right organizing principle for a course at almost any age. But it's also true that teachers know more than their students, and sometimes the most student-centered thing a teacher can do is offer a well-crafted synthesis of a topic or idea. We need to take opportunities to model excellence as well as inquiry. On my team of writing teachers in New York, the teachers would often write with students in response to a prompt, and then share their effort with the class—not to show off higher skill but to enact authentic striving. I loved that teachers were willing to be vulnerable that way but also that they weren't afraid to have students learn things from *their* writing too.

I walked by a science classroom once and, because the door was open, I saw one of my colleagues standing in front of an image of different models for subatomic particles. I was curious and went inside. Students were about to do research projects, but my colleague was framing the work with a mini-lecture that I found captivating. I stood in the back listening until he was done. I couldn't follow the content easily, but I did follow eagerly, because my colleague, very methodically, was able to make the wild world of particle physics engaging. What he was describing seemed like a problem that had to be solved, and he was making the case for its urgency without himself being melodramatic. He wasn't doing the work *for* students; he was making their work possible with his foundational knowledge, and his insistence on the importance of the topic. He was setting up their learning, but he was also sharing what others had already learned, and establishing its gravity.

We've all experienced mind-numbingly dull versions of teachers draining all the life out of the room. The faceless teacher on "Charlie Brown," whose voice comes as white noise buffered with quilts, exaggerates the problem but still gets it right: there's often too much stage, not enough sage. But while honoring the spirit of active, engaged, student-driven learning, we can nonetheless incorporate teacher expertise and dynamism in targeted, smart ways. Imagine an upper grades course that is organized to have an anchor lecture or presentation once a week, or once every two weeks—frequent enough to help synthesize complex work and ideas, infrequent enough to allow student exploration to drive the learning experience. This could also lift the impossible pressure from teachers to produce a great presentation on a daily basis. How about a polished presentation once every two weeks? Or a sharp mini-lecture for ten minutes of a class? Or imagine teams of teachers building units of study together, then dividing up the unit so that each teacher works hard on one home-run presentation. Imagine each teacher devoting her study to one thing, as students benefit from the whole team's efforts. Two of my colleagues in North Carolina did this well. They organized their units to build toward projects, and included research, lots of collaborative activity, and anchor pieces of writing. But they also took a handful of topics to help build the narrative and offer context for what students were learning. For a four-week unit, they each took a couple of topics and crafted fence-post presentations for both classes of students. If it was a unit on medieval travelers, students might be researching a specific historical journey, and the teachers made presentations on travelers who weren't assigned to the kids. They modeled for students how to think about their own topics and also laid common reference points for all the student work. By dividing the labor, and by focusing on a single presentation per week, the chance to do something of high quality increased. Both these teachers reported also spurring each other on, competing in a friendly way to come up with the next new way to make a presentation interesting.

It's striking to me how often in schools devoted to student-centered learning, schools fearful of parading sages on stages, professional development nonetheless involves an outside speaker who lectures or delivers a presentation. I love the good ones every time, and I'm restless during the weak ones. It's the substance more than the form that matters. Students should be exposed to their teacher's knowledge and passion as a spark and catalyst for their own. And teachers need to do a better job making their delivery worthy of their students' interest. They need to cultivate eloquence to go with expertise. If they do, debates about lectures as a form will probably seem beside the point.

Appreciating the form of the lecture shouldn't be controversial in the age of the TED talk. The TED talk is unapologetically a lecture, phenomenally successful lectures at that. After 2006, when the first TED talks were posted, it took only six years for TED videos to reach one *billion* views. And I love many of them. I've shown students portions of TED talks many times. I've used them with teams of faculty. When my New York school was preparing for its opening in 2012, we gathered for a month of work together ahead of time, and a different TED talk was introduced and played before lunch basically every day of training. TED talks follow a consistent, professional format, and the range of topics covered suggests the kind of Renaissance worldview I hope students adopt. I don't want to get all my learning this way. I myself still prefer books to video. But it's a polished, compelling tool, and I'm glad to have that library of talks to access. Schools that admire and use TED talks for their staff should be unworried about the idea of an age-appropriate, expertly executed lecture or presentation as a teacher tool for students.

One of my best teaching experiences involved a summer program run by the state for gifted seniors from across North Carolina. Students selected a major, then, in addition, they all had two required courses, one of which—philosophy—I taught. Both students and faculty lived on the campus of Meredith College, near the fairgrounds in Raleigh. Guest speakers came on a regular basis. Optional field trips were organized. Faculty would offer short elective courses, and students designed other extracurriculars. We also had talent shows and open mics and times for the different majors to exhibit their work. We were a radically student-centered environment, with no grades and few requirements, but with top students pursuing their interests with vigor. Toward the end of the experience one summer, the program director introduced the idea of "lagniappe," a Cajun term, he told us, meaning something extra, a tip, a bonus, a gratuity. He wanted us to offer the students a faculty lagniappe as a gift.

And so, one evening, without telling the students what was going on, we gathered them in the auditorium and just launched into a series of offerings. Our resident poet, a glorious campus elder statesman, stood up in the middle of the auditorium and opened with a recitation of an original poem—as I will never forget. The dance instructors did a marvelous performance to a jagged version of "Moon River." Actors played out a surreal scene. Two colleagues stood on opposite sides of the auditorium and staged a kind of academic dialogue, back and forth, back and forth, on the same topic from the perspective of two disciplines (math and philosophy). It was a collage of offerings but choreographed crisply and with attention to detail. The program director got up at the end and explained "lagniappe" and why we did it. He wanted students to enjoy these parting gifts, he explained, but he also wanted them to see their faculty inhabiting their passions. And you couldn't have accused him or us of not being student-centered, but what he reminded us was that a student-centered program can sometimes park students in

their seats and invite them to watch and listen and learn—
that the demand of self-discipline and attention to other
people is itself a real gift to them. Especially at a time when
we may still over-nurture kids and focus so much on self-
esteem that we forget to cultivate humility and appreciation
for what they don't yet know, and that someone else does.
Student-centered learning doesn't displace the need for deep
faculty knowledge; it steers it. It tells knowledge how to
speak, but it doesn't say, be silent.

"You need not see what someone is doing," the poet
W.H. Auden writes, "to know if it is his vocation,/you only
have to watch his eyes:/a cook mixing sauce, a
surgeon/making a primary incision,/a clerk completing a bill
of lading,/wear the same rapt expression,/forgetting
themselves in a function./How beautiful it is,/that eye-on-
the-object look."

The eye-on-the-object look in teaching can take many
forms. My colleague Dave once reviewed the issues at stake
in the Election of 1860 by being on a one-man, four-
character panel, in which students asked press-conference
questions, and he changed chairs to answer as Lincoln,
Douglas, Breckinridge, or Bell. He and I actually discussed
the approach later. Do you think I should set it up for
students to play those roles? he asked. Maybe, I said.
Probably so, most of the time, but you could also make the
case for a knowledgeable teacher reviewing complex material
with some playfulness. Often when students are presenting,
it's a learning experience for that student or group of students
but a trial of patience for the rest of the class. Sometimes that
tradeoff is the right one. Maybe most of the time. Maybe
not always.

I've known teachers who set the stage for a lecture with
related music as students walk in the classroom. My colleague
Vince would play Hawaiian music and wear leis for his
presentation on Polynesia. I knew a teacher utterly committed

to inquiry-based learning who one day told his students they were going to "play college" today and listen to him lecture on the French Revolution. He was astonished at (and slightly demoralized by) how many students left the room telling him it was the best class they'd had all year. My favorite eye-on-the-object teacher moment occurred in the summer program where we hosted the lagniappe. One day, during free time, a number of us were standing along the quad, and we saw our colleague Rob—Math Rob, as everyone called him—pacing back and forth by himself. A student had presented some math question or puzzle Math Rob couldn't immediately figure out, and he was working it. Head down, Math Rob was pacing back and forth, lost to everything else. He didn't have the solution. One of the teachers I was with called a student over and pointed out what was happening. "I hope someday you have a problem," he said, "that occupies you the way this problem is occupying Math Rob right now." It's the exact right wish for our students. And that was a wonderful, unscripted moment. Math Rob was an unwitting sage on an open-air stage. It took another sage to name it.

THE PROPHETIC SANITY
OF WILLIAM JAMES

So the mind of him whose fields of consciousness are
complex, and who, with the reasons for the action, sees the
reasons against it, and yet, instead of being palsied, acts in
the way that takes the whole field into consideration, so, I
say, is such a mind the ideal sort of mind that we should
seek to reproduce in our pupils.

—— William James

The most lasting legacy of my seminary years was the discovery of the writings of the American philosopher William James. I first read him in a Psychology of Religion class my second year. I'll never forget going out one day to start my car only to discover that the engine was dead. I would either have to miss the psychology class that day or get on my bike and pedal hard for the three or four miles to the main campus. Since I knew the topic that day was James' work *The Varieties of Religious Experience*, I strapped on my backpack, got on my bike, pushed myself, and made it, pouring with sweat, just under the bell.

On a road trip through New England later that same year, in a bookstore near Emerson's house in Concord, Massachusetts, I felt as lucky as a lottery winner: there was a whole row of old hardback volumes of major works by

James, including some first editions. I happily spent money I couldn't really afford. Among that collection was a book not about religion and not about philosophy, my preoccupations at the time, but a book about education: *Talks to Teachers on Psychology: And to Students on Some of Life's Ideals.* I bought that one too. It's sitting by me as I type. When I decided after seminary to become a teacher, that book by William James became a steady companion.

Talks to Teachers is not about curriculum or program or classroom management. If it were, it would no doubt feel dated. Instead, James shares insights from the young field of psychology (the lectures were delivered in 1894) and suggests how they can help teachers teach better. They are surprisingly timeless.

For James, attention is at the core of what it means to think. It was James who coined the phrase "stream of consciousness" to describe the borderless, uninterrupted way we relate to our own experience of the world. Things are always rushing at us, in this view, more than we can process or manage (we are rushing too), and so thinking involves selection and sorting on the move—paying attention to some things and not to others. James harnesses this insight for the classroom. For teachers, the goal is to lure the attention of students to the right things and mobilize their attention in the right way moving forward. It is what in education usually bears the name engagement. James teaches us that prioritizing engagement is rooted in understanding how our minds work. He raises the bar high indeed: "in teaching, you must simply work your pupil into such a state of interest in what you are going to teach him that every other object of attention is banished from his mind; then reveal it to him so impressively that he will remember the occasion to his dying day; and finally fill him with devouring curiosity to know what the next steps in connection with the subject are." If we relieve ourselves of the burden of making every class memorable to every student's dying day, we could helpfully boil down the mission of a classroom along the lines that James suggests: inspire interest in students in important things, then show them what to do next with that interest. Compel their attention, then steer it. It's a pretty good formula.

Having emphasized the importance of winning attention, James reminds us that only the teacher genuinely interested in something can make it engaging to students at all. It is not the loud, performing teacher who wins deep attention. It is the teacher sincerely captivated by something herself. Here is James: "It is useless for a dull and devitalized teacher to exhort her pupils to wake up and take an interest. She must first take one herself; then her example is effective as no exhortation can possibly be." Citing the difference between the "dullness" of one teacher and the "inventiveness" of another, James locates the condition for arousing student interest and attention in the agile attentiveness of the teacher: "One teacher's mind will fairly coruscate with points of connection between the new lesson and the circumstances of the children's other experiences. Anecdotes and reminiscences will abound in her talk; and the shuttle of interest will shoot backwards and forward, weaving the old and new together in a lively and entertaining way. Another teacher has no such inventive fertility, and his lesson will always be a dead and heavy thing." He goes on: "Above all, the teacher must himself be alive and ready, and must use the contagion of his own example…. Elicit interest from within, by the warmth with which you care for the topic yourself."

The teacher must himself be alive and ready. Anecdotes and reminiscences will abound in her talk. The teacher must have *inventive fertility.* How can such things be taught? And how to attract and hold onto teachers with that kind of life inside if we don't begin, as James does, with an insistence that vitality in the teacher is the condition for everything else?

I am a close reader and a long-time fan of both William James and Emerson (who held the infant James in his arms in

81

New York City), but I acknowledge that from a certain angle, exhortations like this can sound either self-evident or sentimental. Emersonian thinking can sound almost too good to be true: Release the student's passion by being passionate yourself. Love what you teach, and your students will love it too. To the skeptic, this can sound a little too much like the power of positive thinking. And maybe so. I've already acknowledged that the artists need the analysts too. But neither Emerson nor James is talking about smiling a lot in class. They are talking about owning what you teach. They are describing the impossibility of shortcuts. They are reminding us that we can't fake our way through a lesson, much less a course.

What we teach has to be inside us, fully internalized, has to mean something to us so that it flows out like a living thing, not something we are trying hard to remember or get right. Here is James' biographer Robert D. Richardson writing about his own college professor, Walter Jackson Bate: "English 10 with Bate was thrilling. I had never encountered anyone for whom literature mattered as much as it did for him. He loved it, all of it. The secret seemed to be to hold nothing back, to care for *all* of it, and to care for what was human in it."

Most students can't resist this kind of all-in commitment, and most are on to insincerity in a flash. They know when a teacher is dialing it in and compensating with charisma or sheer experience. They know the difference between lamplight and fire. For James, teachers have to steal the fire of what they're trying to teach in order to have something with which to ignite actual students. Robert Frost's writing mantra applies: "No tears in the writer, no tears in the reader." No passion in the teacher, no passion in the student. And this is harder than it seems because almost no teacher gets to teach exactly what they want and love—and already have burning inside—but instead have to nourish passion for whatever they've been asked to teach, and are usually asked to

do too much. The high existential bar James sets—or that I'm
setting through James—may be the reason it's hard to achieve
and scale what I'm suggesting we aim for—teaching life,
meeting life with life. But that's the bar, nonetheless. No love
in the teacher, no love in the student.

In terms of specific teaching strategies, James also sounds
wonderfully contemporary. He was way ahead of us in
thinking about what sometimes get called habits of mind.
"The great thing in all education," he writes, "is to make our
nervous system our ally instead of our enemy." To do this,
"we must make automatic and habitual as early as possible, as
many useful actions as we can." A similar focus on building
good mental habits is something that has spawned a whole
subculture in schools. Most schools describe these habits as
dispositions or mindsets that enable the right kind of
learning. Ted Sizer, founder of the Coalition of Essential
Schools, names eight: perspective, analysis, imagination,
empathy, communication, commitment, humility, joy.
Riverdale School in New York City targets seven character
strengths throughout their program: curiosity, gratitude, grit,
optimism, self-control, social intelligence, and zest. My own
school has established high-level thinking skills like empathy,
creativity, and mental agility at the very top of its intended
curriculum. The movement toward this kind of thinking is
consistent with the holistic way James taught us to think
about how we live and learn.

People I've worked with have focused on student habits
and mindsets too. A former colleague organized a humanities
course around the habit of paying attention to detail. The
team liked that emphasis because it transferred easily into
almost any other context a student might experience. It
wasn't so much about discipline expertise or skill mastery as
approaches to the world. An English course attempting to
breed attention to detail is not only trying to develop a certain
kind of close reader but a certain kind of person who
concentrates and sticks with a task, who notices what other

people miss, and who sees concrete particulars of the world not just its frameworks and principles. They began that course with short readings about UCLA basketball coach John Wooden, who launched each season showing his players how to put on their socks and tie their shoes. They included paying attention to detail in writing assignments, in field trip tasks, in media consumption. They had a category on major rubrics devoted to how well the student attended to the details of the work. They built reading units around recognizing significant details in works of fiction and non-fiction. Their students became habituated to thinking about detail and explaining how they honored it in their work.

Another contemporary educational idea that James anticipates is grit. Psychologist and MacArthur "genius grant" recipient Angela Duckworth has made a career advancing the idea that the ability to stick with an interest and see it to its completion is a critical ingredient in successful lives. She calls this quality grit, and its influence among educators is wide and, I think, well deserved. Rereading James' *Talks to Teachers*, I was delighted by his earlier version of grit, which he called *pugnacity*: "We have of late been hearing much of the philosophy of tenderness in education; 'interest' must be assiduously awakened in everything, difficulties must be smoothed away. *Soft* pedagogies have taken the place of the old steep and rocky path to learning. But from this lukewarm air the bracing oxygen of effort is left out. It is nonsense to suppose that every step in education *can* be interesting. The fighting impulse must often be appealed to." How bracing and challenging that call-to-arms is, especially for Romantic-inclined teachers like me. I want everything to be interesting. I want students engaged all the time. But there are days that are just to be gotten through—for teachers and for students. Every teacher knows it's more work to get things organized for a sub than to just show up and fight off your cold. There are days when your very best lesson bombs and days when something you have no confidence in somehow clicks and soars. There are good days ruined by an upset parent's email. There are days when you can't really focus on this very personal job because pressing things in your actual personal life are at the forefront of your mind. There are times when your team makes a choice you don't really love but will support, and it's hard work for you to muster enthusiasm, but you try. Your principal drives you crazy with his stubbornness or incompetence. James adds the need for pugnacity to my insistence on inspiration and life, and it's a realistic reminder from a very generous thinker.

James anticipates other contemporary educational thinking as well, so much so that I'll just recommend the book, which is still in print, and end this lesson. I love William James because his heart is as large as his mind, as a teacher's must be. He was a serious enough thinker to rank as one of America's greatest philosophers, and he was a generous enough thinker to suggest that anything a human being does or finds meaning in is worthy of the philosopher's attention. And I trust James on teaching because he seems to get the balance right between seeing teaching as a science and seeing it as an art form, and I trust him even more because of the affectionate way his own students recalled him. I know teachers get nervous about student evaluations, and I know students need to be trained to offer this kind of feedback well, but it's more than relevant to just listen to students talk about their teachers: It lets us know how our efforts are being experienced. Here is a description of William James by one of his own former students, which would flatter any teacher and which, to my mind, ennobles and reinforces what teachers everywhere are trying to do: "He would then become animated and fluent, with rising assertiveness, and throw off with apparent unconcern the verbal picturesqueness to which his writings have accustomed us. These clarifying interludes were our joy, and James' forte. Positive, even vehement in expression, he none the less impressed us as undogmatic and open-minded, as if science and philosophy were a never-ending but serious game."

WHAT SHOULD WE TEACH?

*I wanted to discover what it was worthwhile for man to do
in the few years he has under the sun.*

—— Ecclesiastes

Now that I'm firmly traveling across the plateau of middle
age, with many more years behind me than lie in front of me,
alas, choices about what I do and read have a calmer, even
sometimes nostalgic quality. I'm not in the hurry I used to be.
I'm still curious and open, and I wonder what I might try to
do next professionally, but the mania to keep up with new
books has dissolved, and while I pay attention to world and
political events, the channel-surfing, link-clicking frenzy of,
say, the person who followed the historic 2008 election like a
paid pundit has released. I'm less concerned with long lists of
things I need to make sure to do, opportunities to consider,
books to read, topics to master. I'm calmer. And as a teacher
too I find myself less worried about what is and is not being
"covered" or taught.

Sometimes I think it doesn't matter really *what* we choose
to teach. The content could be almost anything as long as it's
in the context of vivid, humane encounters between a teacher
fully alive to something—anything—and students who have
woken up to the joy and challenge of something—anything.
Life meeting life, with something interesting happening

between. I'll insist on that as the heart of school at almost any age. It's why you hear people advise college students to find out who the best teachers are and take whatever they offer. The course matters less than the life of the teacher. I like Nabokov's quip: "I doubt whether you can even give your telephone number without giving something of yourself." Great teachers are always giving themselves and their passion away, whether it's through Shakespeare or a shopping list, and the stories people tell about those teachers should be at the heart of how we organize our schools.

And yet still we teach *something*, and we need *some* criteria to determine what that something will be. Students deserve coherent, compelling stories about whatever it is they're learning, and those stories should be connected to their life *now* as much as to future expertise. When I worked on a ten-person humanities team, we used to ask that all our courses tell a story—and that each teacher be able to tell the story of her course. An eighth-grade course focusing on New York City, for example, built the year around two big narratives. Our first framing story was that, like people, cities come of age, and as they do so they experience growth spurts and growing pains. Our second story involved New York as an embodiment of the American Dream, but also, borrowing Langston Hughes' famous image, that same dream deferred. Cities, like people, we told students, are always many things at once—dreams and disappointments, possibilities and failures. We chose those frameworks because they seemed to us to spill over the boundaries of historical study into the realm of actual life. We learned about early New York but by way of thinking about what it means to come of age—as these teenagers were experiencing. The American Dream let us think about aspirations and hopes for ourselves as well as our city. To think of the dream deferred was not only to understand the complexities of our city's history but also to develop empathy for people who experience the world as an uphill battle, and to challenge our conceptions of our own individual dreams. William James said the teacher's job is to "complicate" a natural reaction or "substitute" a different one. We tried to complicate students' understanding of New York—and themselves. It all seemed to us, to use Emerson's image again, commensurate with actual life.

Content choices don't need to be disguised therapies or stealth character education in order to be filled with life. But neither is the content of what we teach only about every discipline's core body of knowledge. I'll say it again: too much of school feels like preparation for more school, and teachers with degrees in their various fields sometimes teach junior versions of their own expertise, and that's it. But curriculum should have what David N. Perkins, in his book *Future Wise: Educating Our Children for a Changing World*, calls a "lifeworthy" quality. He thinks instruction that's driven by bodies of content knowledge ends up in eddies of short-term retention. We need instruction that is more porous to the world outside each discipline: "The hard fact is that our minds hold on only to knowledge we have occasion to use in some corner of our lives—personal, artistic, civic, something else. Overwhelmingly knowledge unused is forgotten. It's gone. Whatever its intrinsic value might be, it can't be lifeworthy unless it's there." He goes on: "Maybe we need to get beyond a presumptive 'good to know.' Knowledge is good to know only if there are occasions that call on it and keep it alive and available. To be worth knowing, knowledge has to go somewhere." Tony Wagner cites the example of students at an elite boarding school being given in the fall a simplified version of a core science final they took the previous spring. In the spring, the average grade was 87%; in the fall, 58%.

Until students decide what they're really interested in exploring, our obligation should be to connect what we teach to the whole variety of lives they will lead. Our classrooms are always full of all kinds of futures, but we sometimes teach as if we want the whole room to choose the career path we chose. The implication of Perkins' lifeworthy criterion is that the aims of every class up to a certain point should be larger than the discipline itself. I think the right time to focus on deep discipline expertise is the point at which students have a choice to opt in or opt out. At that stage, you *are* trying to develop the expertise of your field. Before then, you are provoking interest and engagement, and helping students see how what you're teaching and what you love connects to whole constellations of other things they and other people might love.

In all this, I share Jane Tomkins' lament in her memoir *A Life in School: What the Teacher Learned*: "our education system does not focus on the inner lives of students or help them to acquire the self-understanding that is the basis for a satisfying life." She goes on: "What I would like to see emerge in this country is a more holistic way of conceiving education—by which I mean a way of teaching and learning that is not just task-oriented but always looking over its shoulder at everything that is going on around. Such a method would never fail to take into account that students and teachers have bodies that are mortal, hearts that can be broken, spirits that need to be fed. It would be interested in experience as much as in book knowledge, and its responsibility would be the growth of whole human beings, in harmony with the planet and with one another." I love that line: look over your shoulder at everything that is going on around.

It's easier to agree that young people should know a little bit about coding or be able to speak confidently in front of groups than it is to agree how to educate a heart or a spirit— or whatever you want to call the thing that makes each child worthy of our attention, our respect, and our love. Usually we bracket this aspect of education as belonging to the attitude of the teacher, not what is being taught. I'm suggesting that we not only teach big life questions but frame other things that we teach in their light. Otherwise, we go on making the biggest questions that matter small parts of school life.

Whatever our life is concerned with school should be concerned with: friendship, loss, love, happiness, struggle, justice, change, money, memory, dilemmas, strangers, travel, media, fear, families, wild optimism, crushing pessimism. School should feel like Shakespeare, brimming with life, rather than a test review, tunneling our gaze.

After the unit on The Examined Life my colleague and I improvised to survive our early struggle that year, I started making a list of writing prompts under the same heading. I drew on them for years every so often to have students write reflection papers. And I still fantasize a course or a grade or an entire division of school focused on getting students to think hard about their own life and to take it seriously. The curriculum could be organized around questions like these that flow only from asking students to think hard about themselves and their world:

o What will it look like for you to consider yourself successful?

o What are the biggest obstacles you imagine that will challenge your becoming successful?

o How do you wish other people would describe you?

o How do you think other people misjudge you?

o How do you think you misjudge other people?

o What are you most afraid of?

o How you do think people outside your school view someone like you at your school?

o What do you have in common with people your age in Topeka or Toronto or Taipei or Tehran?

o What's different about your life from people your age in Topeka or Toronto or Taipei or Tehran?

o In what ways would you consider yourself lucky? Unlucky?

o   If you could do anything to make your school environment better, what it would be and why?

o   If you could ask your teachers or your parents to do one thing, what would it be and why?

o   If you could acquire one character trait or virtue that you don't think you have at the moment, what would it be and why?

o   Write about someone you admire and explain why you admire them.

o   If you could trade places with anyone you know, who would it be and why?

o   Describe ways you think computers, the Internet, social media, etc., make our lives better.

o   Describe ways you think computers, the Internet, social media, etc., make our lives more problematic.

o   What are the biggest challenges you see for people your age today?

o   In what kinds of scenarios do you think it's important for people to do things they don't want to do?

o   What are some of the best ways to make sure a community is healthy and strong?

o   Why is it important to have empathy, and are there limits to how much empathy we can have?

o   What are our obligations toward others just because they are human beings?

o   What are the three most important virtues, or character traits, you need to be a good human being?

o   What are the three most important virtues, or character traits, you need to be a successful twenty-first-century citizen?

o   Can we be successful without being selfish?

o   How can we be equal if all of us are so different?

o   Is it harder to be thirteen or thirty-five?

To graduate, you offer a tentative capstone answer to the question in Ecclesiastes about a worthwhile life. We shake your hand. We congratulate you. That's school.

QUIET

Everyone shines, given the right lighting.

— Susan Cain, *Quiet: The Power of Introverts
in a World That Can't Stop Talking*

My first year in New York, I had a student named Marco in my sixth-grade history class. He was shy and pudgy, perfectly polite but also a little aimless, slow on the basketball court, though he wanted to be an athlete. He understood all his tasks and did solid work, but nothing was particularly inspired or memorable. Once, when he got in trouble for some typical middle school misjudgment, I got called to the principal's office as Marco's advisor because he was in there sobbing and needed some support. He didn't come across as an unusually emotional kid or an unusually gifted kid, just a young adolescent with lingering baby fat and the usual developmental anxieties. He wasn't an alpha male who needed to learn humility and compassion. He wasn't the lost kid you worry about who doesn't have any friends. I did what I could to make a connection. He liked basketball. We talked about the Knicks. I worked with him on his writing. He got some A's, mostly B's, and at parent-conferences his parents were pleased with his progress.

Four years on, apparently Marco was doing well. A colleague, who didn't know I'd been Marco's advisor in sixth grade, was complimenting his work, his quiet sense of humor, and a choice he made the other day in class to keep another student from doing something inappropriate. I like Marco, she said. At first he just kind of sat there, but he's warmed up to things, and he gets my jokes, and every so often he'll say something winning.

All told, I must have taught a couple of thousand students across the years, and for a handful of them, I may have been some kind of fork in the road: the right teacher at the right time with the right connection. But the vast majority of those hundreds and hundreds of students I spent long months with have been Marcos. I've paid attention to them and nudged them, laughed with them, challenged them, enjoyed them, worked at their side, but haven't really changed their lives. I've taken care of them, I hope, and put important, interesting tasks in front of them, but most of the time my passion didn't become their passion, and as they progressed down the hall and up the grades, I became one of the seventy or so teachers they would experience before college. Most of those students would find their own way in their own time somehow and be okay, most of their teachers retreating as important but forgotten figures—volunteers who handed them crucial cups of water in the marathon that is school.

When the first group of middle school students that my team in North Carolina taught graduated from high school, we were shocked at the competitive colleges some of the students who had seemed so unpromising were about to attend. Were the college counselors a troupe of magicians? Were the high school teachers that good? What could have happened? We'd been so worried about what some students lacked, and we poured so much effort into filling those gaps, that sometimes, alas, we confused our roles with nature's. Kids just do grow up and figure things out. Not automatically, but also not according to our scripts. We were doing utterly important work on their behalf, but *we* weren't the main thing happening. Growing up was. Year after year, my colleagues and I shook our heads at graduation. Did you see where Ben Yates is going? *That* kid is going to Duke. Amazing. Did you see where Sherry Phipps is going? She could barely write in seventh grade! We marveled at what our students became, pleased for them, proud of them, and in awe of whatever it was we were not responsible for.

All of us collectively created the conditions inside which those kids could figure themselves out. We could see further than they could, after all, so we taught them how to look. We had more experience with obstacles and bewilderment, so we taught them how to solve problems and face ambiguity. We knew interesting books, and we recommended them. We had tricks of the trade in our various fields, and we passed them along. We gave them encouragement, and we offered tough feedback. But what we didn't do was figure out for students how they were going to inhabit their life. Neither did their parents, though a number of them tried. To borrow Alison Gopnik's apt claim one more time: like parents, teachers are gardeners, creating conditions for good growth, not carpenters steaming crooked timber straight.

Teaching humbles you the same way mortality does. It reminds you that your life and your influence follow all the laws of nature. The timetable for each student's growth is different and stubbornly personal. You learn modesty and patience as a teacher. After a while, instead of being frustrated by your limitations, you learn to marvel at this dynamic too. It's a privilege to see an awkward sixth-grader become a poised tenth-grader. There's something moving about seeing growth across the distance of several years—even if, deep down, you wanted credit for big things happening on your watch. It's a privilege to be greeted in the hall by a former student, who seems genuinely glad to see you and who, with a maturity you didn't teach him, asks you questions about yourself and your class and your life. They just do grow up. It's marvelous to see. Lisa Yeager is going *where*? Marco Alvarez wrote *what* about community in his paper? We're participants in life-changing work—catalysts but not the cause. We give our students everything we can while we have them, then very calmly we let them go, and some teacher down the road, when we least expect it of *that* student, gives us a quiet update that makes our day and reminds us that every time they race, at least in Aesop's fable, the tortoise outlasts the hare.

ROOKIE YEAR

I'm not lost for I know where I am.
But however, where I am may be lost.

— Winnie-the-Pooh

I made my way into teaching when I decided not to stay in graduate school, but I didn't have certification, and I had never taken an education course. All I had by way of preparation was a summer internship at an alternative school for at-risk kids in downtown Trenton and a year's worth of apprentice work with a non-profit in New York City that helped place high-performing students from underrepresented groups in private schools along the east coast. I had never properly taught, but I had worked with kids just enough to persuade a small independent school in eastern North Carolina to give me a job as a history teacher. It's probably a good thing no one told me what I was in for.

It wasn't a wealthy place at all. There was no endowment, and tuition was modest, which meant salaries were modest too. My first year's compensation was $23,000. I don't remember what I took home, but our rent for a two-bedroom apartment, I remember, was $575. We needed the second bedroom because my wife was pregnant. For that first year, though, I used the nursery to spread the oversized teacher editions of textbooks on the floor, while, with papers and notebooks all around, I tried to craft a week's worth of lessons at a time every weekend.

I wrote all my lesson plans that year by hand. I had three-ring binders for each course: two sections of 6th grade World History, two sections of 8th grade North Carolina History, one section of 10th grade European History, and one section of 10th grade Public Speaking. The school was small. I taught all the students in those grades. No one collaborated with me. I submitted lesson plans to the head of the upper school and met with him once a week for feedback and advice. Otherwise, I had my five or six classes a day, then club duty (I was volunteered for middle school student government before I knew what that involved), weekly faculty meetings, and, in winter, coaching basketball.

The year was a blur. I knew almost nothing about North Carolina history, and it had probably been middle school since I last thought about ancient river civilizations. So not only did I need to immerse myself in the content of these classes, I also had to figure out how to organize and teach them. As I said, I made it my goal to stay a week ahead of what the kids were doing, and while in good faith I tried to make classes interesting, in reality I was often just synthesizing material in the various text books, delivering that synthesis as best I knew how (lectures, chalkboard notes, short readings and tasks), then giving tests. If I wasn't flailing exactly, I was treading water, and one day, as I did my best with the tenth-grade class, I noticed a student quietly and, I thought, cynically following along in the textbook instead of taking notes. And he was right: I was basically just summarizing what was there. I didn't have the time or capacity to teach all my courses and become expert enough in one to really elevate it. But it embarrassed me to be exposed by a teenager who saw exactly what was going on.

Nothing that I did that year would pass the test of what I consider even satisfactory teaching today. I was a novice, largely learning on my own. I bungled assessments. On the very first tenth-grade test I remember a section of questions asked students to provide both a historical definition of each term but then also connect it to its larger context. When one of the smartest kids in the class read the directions too fast and left out the second half of the task, I docked him twenty points—and put him on his heels instead of working to motivate his obvious intelligence. I didn't know how to do that yet. Studying democracy with eighth-graders, I made the colossally dumb concession that, of course, I couldn't make them stay in class, no one could coerce them, to which a group responded by getting up and walking out. Thankfully, they exercised their newfound democratic freedom to simply lap up and down the hall. After my tenth-graders watched a video of Hitler speaking in the early stages of his political ascent, one of them borrowed a technique we observed in the film for his student government speech. *Hitler.* That student stood in complete silence for a full minute in front of the assembly, the way we had watched the mad man do in Munich. One sixth grade student, after I told the story of the Buddha eating a grain of rice a day, decided to implement that strategy himself at home—as the parents very politely and casually informed me one day when they happened to be at school. Late in the year, I misread the load and the timing with an entire group of students and gave them one project too many, which prompted a different parent to gently persuade me to second-guess a final assignment.

How vulnerable I felt, not knowing, really, how to organize groups of kids to learn anything. And yet there they were, every day, expecting something from me, and I from them, and whatever I tried on a given day would be over like a meal that took hours to prepare but minutes to consume, and I was back to the spare bedroom again that night, and that weekend, to figure out what to do next that wouldn't be too repetitive and predictable.

Meanwhile, there was student government to advise. I'd been given the duty after an initial student government retreat, at which, under someone else's supervision, someone who wouldn't be doing the actual year-long work, they decided their big project would be to paint the bleachers by the soccer field. One of the student's aunts owned a Home Depot-style store and donated the brushes and paint. All that had been decided and arranged by the time I first met with the group. And so, once a week that fall, we hauled supplies out to the field to get the bleachers painted before winter arrived. It was a disaster. The old paint needed a more attentive scraping and sanding than these middle school students could manage. Their approach to the work, understandably at their age, was that volume of paint could cover a multitude of accuracy sins. It was what you'd expect. If I didn't have to do anything afterwards, I'd change clothes and help them paint. Sometimes, though, I was just standing in my work clothes watching and supervising. The amount of paint the kids got on themselves, the jugs of paint thinner we consumed to get them clean enough to go home, the hours and hours it took to finish the job, the way they lost interest too and had to rally each other to try to come, so that some days it would be Meredith and Gray and me, or just noble Gray and me. I celebrated the connections that formed in my second school's Y1K Festival earlier, the bonding that took place while we cut sheets of fake currency or folded programs: this never came close to that effect. Even the kids knew we had bitten off more than we could chew. This was a job for a big group to tackle in a one long day, not a small group to keep changing clothes once a week for an hour. And then the wonderful climax arrived when the athletic director purchased new metal bleachers and pushed our painted benches off to the side. All of it made club day the day I dreaded most in the week, and made rain as welcome as a holiday break. I still get a flashback of trauma at the thought of painting anything.

My other extracurricular was coaching. The athletic director addressed me simply as Coach—as he did every other young male teacher, regardless of their duties. My charge was the middle school boys' basketball team. After the first game, in which I played everybody and tried to give each kid roughly equal amounts of time, the AD called me to his office to make sure I knew we wanted to win. So then I tried to do that too. I remember feeling especially satisfied after one particular game. We'd won a close one and played well, and I thought I'd made reasonably good coaching moves, and with the adrenaline of victory, I went up to the concession area, bought the kind of bright red hot dog you got in that region, and stood along the rail to watch the next game. Various people came over to offer congratulations. I felt tired but relieved at a job well done. And then, at one point, after everyone who wanted to had congratulated me and wandered off, a parent came over to add his congratulations too, except then he kept standing there. He was as quiet and unassuming as his two sons, both of whom I taught. He was looking at the court, not at me, when he said, "You know you got everybody in the game except one player. Were you aware of that?" I tried to review what happened in my mind. The father went on, still not looking at me. "He was sitting at the end of the bench, rubbing his hands together, waiting. I know he's not the best player on your team. Nobody's saying that." He paused. "It's hard when it's your son." Then he walked away. One of the toughest rebukes I've ever taken on the job.

The goodwill of the students—and parents too—was my saving grace. For the most part, students were eager to try things, even as I had to figure out what we should or could even try. In those twilight days of no classroom technology, I tried to coordinate activities with the supervisor of the computer lab. We did what's standard now—we had students prepare PowerPoint presentations—but back then that was cutting edge and monumental. For another project, the sixth-graders brought a video camera in, and we did fake news broadcasts from ancient Rome, which they loved and threw themselves into, almost all of them donning togas and Caesar wreaths as they staged temple scenes and fake weather reports. Austin's outer toga unknotted and slipped off while he slapped at our ancient map with a broken radio antenna pointer. Nicholas, who never missed a question on a test, and who was as polished and polite as a twelve-year-old boy could be, calmly harvested research about Visigoths and Ostrogoths. All of which taught me that you just need to get kids out of their seats and into a challenge, and that you can afford to tolerate the messiness of work if the reward is real engagement, and that the power in a classroom of enjoying each other and an interesting task is not to be underestimated, and how important it is for a teacher to get to see what kind of *people* his students are. One of those sixth-graders, Morgan, stood up in front of the whole middle school to give a student council election speech and paid beautiful tribute to her opponent, an overweight boy who loved history but struggled in school. She thanked him, first of all, for running an admirable campaign and said he would make an excellent vice president, should he win. Her generosity brought tears to my eyes. Another student, Genna, called me Midder Shy and was obsessed with the Beatles and asked me what my favorite Beatles song was, and when I said, "Long and Winding Road" and she didn't want that one, asked for another, and when I said, "Penny Lane," she said, you only like the sad ones. She played Charlotte in the local theater company's production of *Charlotte's Web*, and she was so marvelous, and so dynamic, and when she wasn't speaking, she stayed active in her makeshift web, moving her hands as if she were knitting. I sent her a card the next day. It said only "Bravo!" I meant it as speechless tribute. She came in, wonderfully rebuking me: "That's all? One word? That's all I get?" She brought energy to every class and always wanted to know what we were doing next and was it going to be fun and could we dress in costumes and bring in props and did I think she'd get an A and was I considering Genna as a name for the baby my wife and I were about to have. At the end of the year, I got to give one award to a history student in each grade, and Genna knew it and asked me about it, and it did and didn't matter to her, she wasn't grubbing for it, she just had really loved the class and given it her all, and who was more enthusiastic than she was, she rightly asked. I told her no one. I said I'd give her a shelf of awards if I had them, but then we talked and she agreed that it would mean the world to Austin to get this kind of recognition, because school was harder for him than it was for her, and he loved history too, and the little plaque, in the end, went to him, and Genna celebrated that marvelously. She was always going to be okay, and she knew it, and she was. Early years of teaching, I suspect, get marked by those students who, while you're figuring things out and are being snowed under and defeated on a regular basis, make you love the work anyway. Genna did that for me.

I got to school early, determined to be fully prepared. I was usually the third person to arrive, parking my ageing Subaru station wagon in the same spot every day, beside Paul's Silverado pickup truck and Philip's dented Nissan. Ahead of me, one of them would have made the first pot of coffee, and sometimes we found ourselves together there for the brewing of pot two. Philip and I laughed when we discovered that Paul, a sixty-year-old smoker who looked like he might have been eighty, simply poured new grounds onto the old grounds to make the second batch. It must have been straight frugality. It had the whiff of mischief. The early stillness in the school before students—and most teachers— arrived was almost sacred. And we were like people from older times getting up before dawn to do farm chores, and when dawn breaks, you've already accomplished something. We spent a few minutes around the coffee machine, waiting for Paul's hybrid brew. I remember how he tested us too to see what kinds of jokes we would laugh at. Would we join light mockery of the new admissions director? Would we side with the new head of school, who wasn't from around here, or would we line up with the old guard? And would we listen to Paul and other lifers when it came time for the rookies to defer? We filled our mugs. We went separate ways. I crossed the open quad between our buildings.

The school year was almost over. I walked in pants I remember buying at Macy's on sale, right before we moved south for the job. I wore a white shirt and a tie from Jos. A. Bank, where my father-in-law shopped. I'm walking, holding a mug with a Far Side cartoon, and feeling a mixture of calm (because I'd prepared) and anxiety (because you never knew how the kids would respond) and hopefulness too, because for all the feeling of being exposed I was figuring things out, little by little, and even though it took me three years to feel competent and confident, and even though I had plenty of sophomore mistakes ahead, I wasn't where I was when I started, and the kids were all right. Anyway, who knew what crazy thing Genna would ask if we could do as a class that day, and who knew if it was going to be more like that day a frustrated student got up and just walked out of class to calm down because other things were going on in his life or the day a different student woke up to the startling opening of *A Portrait of the Artist as a Young Man* and decided, on her own, to read the whole book.

MS. ACUFF

Not knowing when the Dawn will come,
I open every Door.

—— Emily Dickinson

Cognitive research goes on showing us how many tricks our brains play on us (or themselves). Daniel Kahneman's bestselling *Thinking, Fast and Slow* is a portrait of how our mind edits our experience. We trust repeated stories over discoverable facts, for example, and unconsciously substitute simpler questions when faced with something too hard. What observer of contemporary politics would dispute this? Even memory is not an archive preserving footage of our life so much as an active, invested storyteller, reimagining lost experiences selectively. It's not mischief or ignorance; it's just being human.

Which gives me pause. My insistence on the romance of teaching relies on anecdotes and portraits because that's how people relate their formative experiences of school. I know I do. But if memories and anecdotes are unreliable, and we know how prone we are to recast complicated experiences in simpler, hopeful terms, shouldn't someone concerned with setting students up for success resist getting suckered by a myth-happy mind? Shouldn't I mistrust imagination, or at least surround it with rational sentries, check my belief in the role of inspiration with progress reports and reading levels and standardized tests? At the end of the day, doesn't data tell me more about a school really than the impressions of parents or the accounts of former students?

I grew up in an Appalachian town of 20,000 residents on the Virginia-Tennessee border. North of us were coal towns, hidden in the mountains. South, you crossed more mountains into North Carolina. Down in our little valley, my father worked as a production manager in local plants, one of which made compressors, the other hospital supplies. Older American work. The public high school I attended had about a thousand kids. There was a clutch of serious students, to be sure, but that wasn't the dominant group. A modern, expansive vocational wing was just as important to the life of the school as the A.P. classes. I took typing in the vocational wing, in a room filled with so many typewriters it must have looked, when we were clacking through our drills, like one of those code-breaking bunkers in a World War II film.

In my ninth-grade year, I learned I needed glasses because I couldn't read the filmstrip caption up on the screen in Biology I. Mrs. Harrenburg looked at me over her glasses. You can't read that? she said. Usually stern, she seemed suddenly sympathetic. I never loved science, but we got to dissect things in Biology I. We dissected a worm. It had an eraser-sized gland whose name begins with a "c." Capellum? It does something. In ninth grade, I learned to spell forty. On all the drafts of a paper I handed in, I kept writing "fourty," and the teacher kept circling it, and I was sure she was mistaken, until, finally, I looked it up and learned to spell forty. I played basketball that year and ran cross country. We used to get up at 5:30 to run before school. In the locker room after, I drank a thermos of grapefruit juice and ate some power bar my mother was selling, along with vitamins, to try to make some extra money, now that my father had moved out. In ninth grade, Reagan was shot. One of the runners on the team raced up to tell me at the bottom of a hill we were about to take. In ninth grade I hit puberty, and it was about time because almost everyone had beaten me to it, and it's no fun to be that boy in a high school locker room. In tenth grade, my father opened a restaurant on a rural highway. It failed miserably and cost him his second marriage. In tenth grade, my math teacher sat on a stool right beside the overhead projector and wrote out problems on those transparent sheets that showed the shadow of her hand and the shadow of her pen and impossibly neat handwritten problems spilling from those silhouettes. In tenth grade, I took driver's ed. The athletic director in charge of the training smoked cigars in the car as he drove us to the practice course. In tenth grade, Mike Lane was called on to read aloud the Robert Frost poem "Birches" in our textbook, and he read it so badly, so flatly, I remember wanting to interrupt and demand that someone else—I probably wanted to do it—be given a chance to put some music and life into it. I remember that. I can even summon the poem's elegiac opening. In tenth grade, I didn't know what I wanted. I knew I wanted to go to college, but I wasn't thinking at all about where. I must also have taken the PSAT. I don't remember my score. It didn't earn any kind of citation or award. In tenth grade, my older brother moved to West Virginia to finish high school and live with my grandparents. My mother's sister, who lived there too, announced that he had a girlfriend, and when we all went up for graduation, my father took a picture of this girl as she came off the stage, and she looked at him guardedly, and he told her he was my brother's dad, and she just walked on. They had broken up long before. When I was in tenth grade, that same brother signed up for the Air Force. We drove him to the bus station rather than the airport. In tenth grade, in the middle of all that, I checked out a library copy of *The Catcher in the Rye* and, when I opened it in study hall later that day, I felt a leap of attention so quick and unexpected it was like picking up a book in another language and realizing I understood every word. I couldn't have said exactly what it was I discovered (that the secret of great writing is voice?), but I read the book straight through—and then read it again right after. In tenth grade, my father tried to get me to read *Summerhill*, a book about a British school that gave students the kind of freedom he himself went on craving in his own life.

In eleventh grade, I wrote for the student newspaper and played varsity basketball. In eleventh grade, I quit the basketball team because it looked like I wasn't going to get any kind of real playing time, but, when he found out, my junior high basketball coach came to my house and told me I needed an outlet, needed to be involved in something, and managed to talk me out of quitting. In eleventh grade, my older brother finished basic training and was sent to Germany. In eleventh grade, my younger brother started playing football. In eleventh grade, I used to wake up early and read the paper every morning with my toast, but I'd have to do some research to tell you what the big stories were that fall or the following spring. In eleventh grade, we watched Sports Center while we waited for my mom to get ready for work and to drop us off at school on her way. In eleventh grade, four of my friends got cars. And in eleventh grade, I had an English teacher, Annette Acuff, who, without any fanfare, changed my life by handing me books, the most important teacher I ever had.

Our English class met in a ground-floor room with four rows of desks attached to their chairs. Wire baskets beneath the desk stored your books. Green chalkboards lined the front wall. A flag in its little bracket rose beside a speaker that let the office call in if a student was being dismissed. To the right, windows faced a narrow space between buildings. On the top of the cupboards along the near wall were stacks of novels we would read that year: *The Scarlet Letter*, *Moby-Dick*, *The Great Gatsby*.... There was a bulletin board too. Every classroom had one. Some of the teachers filled them with elaborate rotating displays. Ms. Acuff didn't do much with hers. I wouldn't have either.

She liked to sit up front on a stool, drinking coffee. I see
her there in my mind's eye with a sweater over her shoulders.
I think at the time I thought she was older than she was.
Because she didn't go by Missus, we knew she wasn't
married. Like so many of the teachers, she sometimes hurried
to the faculty lounge between classes to sneak a smoke. She
was quiet and monotone, a Transcendentalist (I would learn)
living in the Appalachian Mountains. As teachers of previous
generations did, she had impeccable cursive penmanship. Her
comments at the end of our papers were elegant paragraphs
that modeled good prose, not the whip-strike notes I
sometimes still slap on student papers.

And I doubt Ms. Acuff stood out to most students when
they told stories to their families at night, or when, years later,
they thought about high school. She didn't have a reputation
that made me look forward to having her in class that year.
The line on 11th grade A.P. English was that Ms. Acuff would
teach you how to write long essays, and also you got to read
pretty good books. But early in the year I remembered being
bored, and while our class crept through the canon of
American writers, starting with the Puritans, I started flipping
to the back of the big anthology we had to see the kind of
work we would never get to in our chronological quest, the
Hemingways, the Eliots, the Sylvia Paths and Robert Lowells.
And in that aimless reading, I came across a Lowell poem
that began this way:

It was a Maine lobster town—
each morning boatloads of hands
pushed off for granite
quarries on the islands,

and left dozens of bleak
white frame houses stuck
like oyster shells
on a hill of rock

Sitting in the back of that English class, hiding and, to be honest, curling around a cynicism I think now was an imitation of my father's, I read that poem over and over, and something rose in me, and it was a little like my experience with *Catcher*—I didn't know writing could be like this: the ease, the intimacy, the achievement of atmosphere, the houses like oyster shells, an image I've never forgotten—to go from John Greenleaf Whittier to this. I stayed in the back of the book from that day forward, reading whoever else was there, looking for more of what I vaguely intuited, and Ms. Acuff must have known what I was doing. I must have said something to her. I can't recall. She must have lectured the class on occasion, though I don't remember anything specific she said. She loved Emily Dickinson and read her poems aloud, and she loved Emerson and Thoreau, and so when we got there in the book we took our time with them, and she had us write journals in the Transcendentalist style—thirty days, thirty entries, nature-themed with self-reflection—and meanwhile, as we learned how to write an analytical essay, she spotted something going on with me and started giving me books to read after class. I devoured them. And that was how she changed my life. Very quietly, very discreetly, that's how Ms. Acuff became for me a fork in the road.

One winter day she loaned me a collection of short stories by Thomas Wolfe, who was from Asheville, two hours away, just across the mountains. My basketball team had a road game that night. Our ritual was to drive over to Hardee's after school, eat burgers as a team, drink Cokes, then settle into the school bus for the one-or-two-or-three-hour ride. I was sitting near the front of the bus as we headed toward one of the coal towns deep in the surrounding mountains. And I had that book. And because the days were short, to read I had to hold the book high to catch remnants of afternoon light. The bus had no heat; the window was creek cold. The spine of the book was dry and cracked. Ms. Acuff couldn't have opened it for many, many years. I turned the borrowed pages with gloved hands, shutting out as best I could the rival boom boxes in the back rows: the Sugar Hill Gang, the Boy George, the Van Halen. A chaperone sat between the cheerleaders and the players. The narrow mountain roads were white with winter salt, and little clusters of clapboard homes tucked against the rocky slopes like the oyster shells in Lowell's poem. Smoke from the chimneys, clean wood smoke, dissolved in the gathering night. On porches were unboxed stacks of logs; in driveways, pickup trucks and American cars. Our coach was driving the bus. A big man, a former college player, he wore turtlenecks beneath his blazers for our games and bought oranges by the bushel for us to eat after practice. When he glanced up from the road now, his eyes in the enormous rearview mirror were like the billboard eyes in *Gatsby*. I leaned close to the cold window, adjusting my book to the passing light. Everything felt alive, everything lay exposed, available. Ms. Acuff had held me back after class. She thought I might like these strange stories. And they were strange, and intoxicating, stories about Brooklyn and men wandering New York, a city I hadn't yet visited but would one day live in, and they were inundated with impressions, and Wolfe was barely able to contain and manage the language. Is how it seemed to me then. The prose had the kind of shapeless, abundant energy that I was beginning to feel inside, the shapeless gift of freedom that felt not like the world really is but the way we necessarily experience it, too much all at once, not irrational—unsorted, excessive, spilling over anything attempting to contain it. What I experienced in those stories, I think, was that, through writing, the pressure weighing on a life could be released as well as contained. It could adopt a shape. Pressure could yield a vision, not just a threat. You could receive the pressure and then make something of it, even if it didn't set you free. You could get somewhere by submitting yourself to what it was, even if you weren't sure exactly what you meant by your allegiance. You wanted something to be loyal to more than you wanted escape. It felt like love of the world. Like seeing through an extra lens. Like religion without the burden of theology. And it was relief from the pressure that sent my older brother away and the pressure clearly weighing on my parents in different ways. Every life is too much, as everybody discovers. But if you're lucky you find something that sorts other things away. What school is *for*.

I read until the mountains closed out the light, and with my head against the cool glass, I wanted to just ride on, tracing the remote towns, drifting through the winter dark, the cheerleaders with their matching pleats, the boom boxes choked with batteries, our coach with his window down as he smoked, letting in the mountain cold. Our best player, Kevin, sat close to the front on the way, to get himself ready for the game. I sat near the front with a different preparation in mind.

The whole night comes back: the cold locker room where we changed quickly and where my friend Danny dug around in the trash cans for candy bar wrappers because if you saved fifty, or however many it was, you could mail them in for five dollars. Holding a clipboard, our coach talked us through the scouting and the strategy. Outside the locker room, cheerleaders made a shivering arcade of pompoms. We ran under that arch into an old gym whose bleachers were pulled close to the court, and the humid noise of the crowd joined with opposing cheerleaders and a pep band surrounding us. Doing layups, we looked back at the other team to take their measure. Big mountain boys banged hard, but we were faster, and Kevin was the best player in the region. I scored seven points off the bench that night, which was good for me. The game came to me, as they say, and even that was like a confirmation. On the ride home I couldn't read, it was too dark, but I held the Wolfe in my lap regardless because, even closed, it went on offering something that felt like a promise, like a secret that would never abandon me.

Almost forty years later, as I was working on this book, I
was in the Strand Bookstore on Broadway in Manhattan,
browsing for nothing in particular, and in the course of
browsing I saw a few books by Thomas Wolfe, and I took
them off the shelf and held them and felt the release of old
associations again—I hadn't been looking for them at all—
and it was wonderful, even if it was quick and passing.

To give a student something that will live on inside that
way, to offer a student moments and encounters that turn
their course and set them on a path they feel, decades later,
they've never quite left, to break seams of light in early
darkness is the highest privilege of a teacher. Who else gets to
do this? And even if it's an accident when and how it
happens, it's not incidental; it's not secondary to the real work
of teaching. The sun is the sun. Let planets orbit where
they can.

Did Ms. Acuff show me how to write? She must have. We
wrote those essays. Did she teach me how to read a complex
text? Within her range she must have done. But over time I
figured both those skills out in the way I needed them,
because I had an appetite for language and its forms and
surprises. I wanted books, and I wanted writing, and I figured
my way toward them—and still try to. And you can decide
whether you think a young person needs to get all the skills
down first before they can really wake up to possibilities or
whether waking up to possibilities *is* the work, and teachers
are facilitators, readers of young lives, and givers of
themselves and what they know, or like Walt Whitman,
another writer Ms. Acuff admired, hooking an arm around
your shoulder and pointing toward but not walking for you
the Open Road.

ALMOST TEACHERS

We teach who we are. Good teaching requires self-knowledge: it is a secret hidden in plain sight.

— Parker J. Palmer, *The Courage to Teach*

Even for the church-going region I grew up in, my grandfather's version of religion was extreme. He was a Baptist minister with congregations so small and remote they could barely pay him a salary. And so, after he and my grandmother moved to be near us, he always had part-time jobs to supplement his meager church income. For a long time, he picked up camera film from local retailers, drove the packets to a developing lab, received finished prints from the day before, and returned them to the various stores. An aggressive driver, he talked his way out of speeding tickets by announcing himself a Man of the Lord.

He had other jobs too, but it wasn't until his funeral that I remembered or even became aware of his stint teaching at a small Christian school. My mother nudged me to turn around in the pew. At the back of the church, wearing school uniforms, about a dozen kids filled a row, waiting for the service. My mother whispered in my ear that his students really loved him. And it's so memorable to me because no one in our family was ever close to my grandfather. Everyone's relationship with him was difficult. I think my mother said what she said, in part, to defend him at his funeral, or to salvage something like an achievement to his credit when every one of his real family connections was so strained.

My grandfather lived like a recluse. He had diabetes. I saw him once giving himself a shot of insulin in his pale hip. Whether he really was as fragile as he seemed or just lazy, he lay on his bed most of the day, even when we were visiting, did his church work in his room, and came out in pajamas and slippers only to get snacks or to ask my grandmother to make him a sandwich, so defined and traditional and inflexible were their roles.

Because I had an eight-year stretch of my own of fairly intense religion—right after he died, as it happened—I became interested, as an adult, in my grandfather's life. Cassette tapes of his sermons reveal someone emotionally volatile in the pulpit. He preaches about the joy of being a Christian while sounding like someone under tremendous duress. Describing our standing before God if we don't respond to the gospel, he shouts like someone putting an end to all arguments: Guilty! GUILTY! In one sermon, he offers a strange throwaway comment about making love to his wife (he and my grandmother slept in separate rooms and lived a kind of truce), and in another his voice grows angry as he tells his tiny congregation, none of whom had money, that if they weren't tithing, they were stingy and, worse, were robbing Gaaaahhhhddd. This intensity and hostility in the pulpit matches the descriptions of his own children about growing up with my grandfather. My uncle tells of how my grandfather turned on him once and announced that he was going to split the gates of hell wide open—because he had set a box down in the wrong spot. The same uncle was riding in the passenger seat once when my grandfather slammed the brakes. My uncle's head hit the windshield and cracked it; my grandfather was upset about the glass. My grandfather and my father were always at odds. My father told stories of my grandmother standing in front of my father's bedroom door to protect him from my grandfather's intrusion. My grandfather once spit in my grandmother's face. When my aunt married a Catholic, my grandfather would not attend the wedding.

He was disturbed and lost to himself, I think, and yet, though I glimpsed all these things, and he died essentially estranged from his children, with us grandchildren he was different. He did urge us toward religion, giving us books with long, theological inscriptions, and taking us on our twelfth birthday to the Bible store downtown to pick out an expensive leather Bible (I still have mine). But he could be more relaxed and playful too. His diabetes limited his movement, but he'd go out back when we played whiffle ball, and he would take a turn hitting and let one of us run for him. He came to most of our little league baseball games. The image that lingers in my mind is of my grandfather standing at the right field fence, away from the crowds in left and center, wearing his short sleeve dress shirt and clip-on tie, drinking coffee from a thermos cap, and watching us play. He'd leave right after the games. He didn't come to congratulate or comment.

Those kids in Christian school would have gotten that softer version of my grandfather, not the strident pulpit one. And if my mother is right and they loved him, I can't help thinking he would have been happy and effective and even great as a teacher full time, relieved of religion, or at least religion's duty to compel people into its version of a Kingdom. People divided against themselves can get eaten alive in a classroom. I've seen it. Kids test their teachers and press their own advantage. I've known a handful of teachers personally who were just too shaken by the job to stay in it. It takes confidence and poise to steer a room of kids. But at some level caught people, even lost people like my grandfather, can make powerful teachers because the tension they experience inside can lead to compassion for kids trying to make their own difficult way. And people with knots and ambiguities inside are practiced in the art of trying to figure things out, and make them clear. Teacher skills.

My father was a teacher for one year in a West Virginia school as remote as my grandfather's church. He had one student, he said, who was interested in larger things, was interested (this would have been 1965) in Bob Dylan, and that bonded them. But then he got a job offer to move to North Carolina and work in industrial management, and the money was too good, many times more than he was making as a teacher, and he had two kids to raise now (hello, me), so he took it, and left teaching behind forever. And he was successful for a while but never really happy in the business world. After my parents divorced, he tried operating that small barbecue restaurant, but it went south fast, and after declaring bankruptcy and after getting a second divorce, he disappeared for a while, and when he reemerged, he took one last business job before quitting again. His third wife was a nurse. As I finished college, my father went to nursing school so they could pick up and move easily, which they did for a long time, east to west, west to east, over and over.

My father was as least as unsettled as my grandfather, and like my grandfather he became estranged from his own kids. And like my grandfather, a part-time, informal teaching stint showed my father in maybe his best light: for five years, he became a wildly successful little league baseball coach, and in thinking of him in that role, I see the most relaxed, organized, also joyful version of him I can recall. He was his best self as a teacher, a coach.

What made him a great baseball coach? He was, first, a student of the game. When he took on the task, he started reading instructional books. The one I remember best was Ted Williams' guide to hitting. He built a system around our practices, so that pitchers were throwing fifty practice pitches every other day, and every hitter every time we met got twenty hits at the plate. We also practiced game scenarios, and like a good teacher, he offered a principle—throw ahead of the runner; start moving a little as the pitch is thrown—then he had us practice doing it over and over. He was building habit and muscle memory without giving it a name. I remember one time he and my brother and I were watching Monday Night Baseball, and he went to the phone between innings, like a manager calling the bullpen, to tell the left-handed pitcher on our team to turn the game on and watch how high this pitcher was kicking his leg. When we had games, he kept meticulous records, and he handed out Xerox copies of our statistics once a week. As my father outthought everybody in the league, we won four straight championships.

One year he took an all-star team to the state finals. I don't remember him so happy, so free. He organized charts of statistics and presided over practices in which all the parents for the all the all-stars sat in the bleachers watching the team—watching him. Those practices were full of scenarios: He'd put runners on bases, and say to his defense, okay, runners on first and third, nobody out, does everybody know what to do? They'd register the scenario, then he'd hit a ground ball, or a pop-up, or lay down a bunt, and he'd watch the defense react. Then they'd go over what everyone had done and who needed to do something differently, then they'd run the play again. Then he'd switch it up: runners on first and third, but two outs this time. Then maybe he'd quiz players on what they'd do if the ball came to them. Then he'd hit a ground ball or a pop up, or lay down a bunt. When we won the district tournament that year, he and an assistant coach, and both our families stayed up late at their house celebrating, and at two or three in the morning we went to a truck stop to get breakfast food because by this point he'd decided to just stay up all night until the paper was delivered so we could read about the game and relive its tense, 2-0 triumph. He loved his young players especially, the ones who weren't all that good. He laughed easily at the kid who always complained hard at his glove on a botched play, or the kid who pulled his hat way down over his eyes and kept his pockets stuffed with ruler-sized bars of Tangy Taffy, which seemed the real reason he was even playing. My father had fun with every aspect of coaching, but meanwhile he taught us the intricacies of the game, kept studying the game himself to get better, more knowledgeable, and when we made mistakes he used them as opportunities for instruction not for rebuke: in practice we'd go over plays that hadn't gone well in previous games, work on how to do it differently the next time. He drove kids home if they didn't have a ride. If we were going to get food, that kid got food too. When he came home from work, he'd ask if we'd thrown our pitches. On summer vacations, we went to major league games. He was all-in, passionate and expert, large and generous. He made his good players great by practicing the right things over and over; he made the kids who were really just there to have fun not feel like they were in our way. He enjoyed them too and didn't put pressure on them to be what they weren't. He told one kid once to "take until you get a strike," which meant, don't swing until the pitcher gets a strike on you. The kid swung at the first pitch he saw—and missed. After two more strikes, he jogged back to the bench. My father: "Kevin, I said, take until you get a strike." Kevin: "It was a strike." My father chuckled, acknowledged the possibility of Kevin's logic, and just waved him back to the bench. He'd go over the intended logic next time. Kevin, anyway, had another ruler of taffy to consume. My father was an ideal coach for both the superstars and for the Kevins, and an ideal teacher this way, pushing for excellence but enjoying each kid for whoever he was.

Soon after my last brother moved on from little league, my father moved on too: a new marriage, the money-pit restaurant, bankruptcy, and, over time, a restless moving around the country that took its toll on him and everybody around him, so that he ended up more like my grandfather than he would want to admit. In his final years, we didn't talk very much. My other brothers and he didn't talk at all. He died under extraordinarily sad and tragic circumstances.

But he was that coach once too, as good a teacher as I've known. And it's not lost on me, though it also wasn't intentional, that for the bulk of my career I taught 7th grade, which was the grade I was entering when my father moved out.

AFFIRM SOMETHING

My project rises from delight, not disappointment.
— Toni Morrison, *Playing in the Dark*

One way to read the world we've inherited is to say that everything that was once assumed to the be the case now has to be argued for and established as the case. Nineteenth-century thinkers did the work of registering this for us: "All that is solid melts into air," wrote Marx. Nietzsche's version: "What did we do when we unchained the earth from the sun?" Later, Virginia Woolf told us that human character itself changed "on or about December 1910," and Einstein, sure that the universe was orderly, was flummoxed by unpredictable quantum physics. Copernican revolutions make you stay on your toes.

The other way to describe this inheritance is to say that the freedom we now assume to be ours is both windfall and burden. It asks us to create meaning ourselves rather than receive it from somewhere else. Lucky us: we get to find our own way. Nobody else charts our path for us. Lucky us: we have to find our way. Nobody has a map in his pocket with our name on it.

Kwame Anthony Appiah summarizes this condition neatly in *The Ethics of Identity*: "Each of us has one life to live; and although there are many moral constraints on how we live our lives—prominent among them being constraints that derive from our obligations to other persons—those constraints do not determine which particular life we must live.... There are also constraints on how we may live that derive from our historical circumstances and our physical and mental endowments.... But even when we have taken these things into account, we know that each human life starts out with many possibilities. Some people have a wider range of options than others.... But everybody has, or should have, a variety of decisions to make in shaping a life. And for a person of a liberal disposition those choices belong, in the end, to the person whose life it is." Appiah calls this "our life making." For me, great teaching involves assisting and nurturing young students in *this* quest, not just in helping them get ready for a daunting job market.

I don't want to prescribe meaning for students, and I don't want to misuse my position to suggest what kinds of meanings and commitments students should make. I don't think I have those answers for them. I'm willing to say that I want them to encompass as much as they can in their thinking, in their feelings, in their budding worldviews. I want them to be good and decent people, also reasonably happy but still curious and maybe even a little restless. I want their heads up, taking in the world. I want them to feel like discoverers. I hope they love well and help bend the long arc of the universe toward justice and compassion.

But how do teachers care about the larger building of a life without playing the part of priests and politicians? My provisional answer is to say that teachers need to affirm something about life and even about the world, that it's not enough to give students tools for critical thinking without also inspiring them to embrace and love something deeply. I take Tolstoy's comment about the role of art to be true of the role of the great teacher: *make people love life in all its countless, inexhaustible manifestations.* Not uncritically, not dogmatically, not sentimentally, and yet surely. We have to help students make a life, not just get through school. If nothing else, taking that quest seriously in school and having teachers name and value and explore it is the courageous—and difficult—thing to do. It's difficult because it's hard to affirm things period anymore—in or out of a classroom. Every understanding requires nuance. Every explanation can be deconstructed, every commitment qualified. Every claim or idea can be peeled back until, like an onion, you see that there was nothing ever there except the layers you thought protected a deeper truth. It's tempting, especially with older students, to think the job is to cast light on the limitations, the impossibilities, and the relentless struggles, even as it's tempting, with younger ones, to assume the end of what we're doing in school is so straightforward: preparing informed citizens who have skills to land twenty-first-century jobs. Maybe the balance is something like this: teachers need to bring something they want to share and incite in their students. But teachers can't try to duplicate themselves in their students. "You are trying to make that man another you," Emerson said, chiding overeager educators. "One's enough."

The route to real affirmation, I think, passes through skepticism and doubt. Some of our most affirming thinkers struggled with despair. "Schopenhauer, though a pessimist, really," Nietzsche wrote, "played the flute." And who is more ambivalent than Chekhov, who with one hand traces the final oblivion surrounding us and with the other hand spots ennobling lights in the dark? In his story "Lights," Chekhov has a young student look past the progress and energy of a railway being built to the quieted fate that awaits everyone. Like ancient biblical tribes, he says, all the people standing here will become forgotten dust. "You must drop those thoughts," an older engineer tells him. "Thoughts like that are for the end of life, not for the beginning of it. You are too young for them." The student presses, and the engineer goes on: "All these thoughts of the transitoriness, the insignificance and the aimlessness of life, of the inevitability of death, of the shadows of the grave, and so on, all such lofty thoughts, I tell you, my dear fellow, are good and natural in old age when they come as the product of years of inner travail, and are won by suffering and really are intellectual riches; for a youthful brain on the threshold of real life they are simply a calamity! A calamity!"

Teachers, don't read this to your students. They're not the audience for it. You are.

Without effort, students today will encounter skeptic after skeptic. The curtain will be pulled back on every conviction. Mentor after mentor can show them how to doubt. The rarer influence will be the figure who, having learned all the necessary skepticism, nonetheless sings and affirms. Maybe a different time will cry out for even more cynicism still. Maybe we'll get too soft and sentimental. Maybe we'll need our illusions punctured with darker narratives. Maybe we'll look past our faults and blind spots in dangerous ways again. We seem to have a beat on those now, and it may be more pressing—or at least as pressing—for students to see models of how you build and construct and hope and create in spite of our limitations. On a practical level, we might do more with biographies—real life stories, so that as students learn about collective atrocities and systematic missteps, they see ways that individual human beings struggle inside every possible condition to do great and noble things, as well as repugnant and shameful ones.

Like everyone else on January 20, 2021, I was deeply moved when twenty-two-year old Amanda Gorman stood at the podium on the Capitol steps and read her poem at the presidential inauguration. In a context and in a location in which anger would have been understandable and even justified (more than 20,000 National Guard had gathered to secure the event, two weeks after the Capitol riot), this young poet summoned all of our better angels, and with bravery and candor affirmed something large. It was inspiring. It's getting harder and harder to inspire—for philosophical reasons, not just political ones. It's bracing to experience fresh examples of it. We teachers don't want to tell students what to think or what to love, but we do want to create conditions in which students, equipped with all the tools of critical thinking and historical understanding, can nonetheless affirm something. Amanda Gorman's teachers should be proud.

VIRTUES OF GREAT TEACHERS

*Better to say, when I'm reading this book, I believe it, with
my whole soul. It allows me to say things I wouldn't
normally. Things like 'She is my sister and I love her.'*

— Zadie Smith (on reading Zora Neale Hurston)

I don't want to downplay the ordinary qualities that make up
any good teacher. Cars can be fun to drive but mostly they
need to run and run reliably. The brakes need to work. The
doors need to close. The heater needs to blow. Teachers need
to be reliable, confident, fair, consistent, hopeful, and firm. I
don't want to suggest only glinting chrome fins matter. The
teacher I claim as the most important in my own life, after all,
was anything but charismatic. I see her sitting on her stool
with a cardigan over her shoulders. She's holding coffee to
warm her hands. She has a green grade book for recording
attendance. She has a lesson on the board. Her handwriting is
from an era when penmanship mattered. *That* teacher
changed my life. So, as I set out to describe some virtues of
great teachers, I'm not thinking of the way they run a class so
much as the kind of person they are in the room—what they
bring to the job.

Is there a rubric for what constitutes a great human being?
If so, use that rubric to describe a great teacher. We don't
have a script for what students should become. We shouldn't

have one for teachers either. Maps maybe, but not scripts. And if I'm not trying to oversell glitz, I am trying to say something unexpected about teachers. Not as a way to get a rubric right but as a way to push the boundaries back to make room for a fuller portrait of what a teacher is and does. The job needs people with big hearts and minds, but big imaginations most of all. Portraits of teachers, then—job descriptions—should make people see teaching as a place for the most talented, ranging minds around, even if, to our shame, they're not paid accordingly—with respect or with money.

I said earlier that telling someone you're a teacher should elicit the same response as telling them you're with Doctors without Borders. But it doesn't. Norwegian writer Karl Ove Knausgaard, looking back on a year as a young teacher, complained: "I was a *teacher*, was there anything sadder than that?" Actually, sir, yes. Very many things. And in his standup routine, the comedian Louis C.K. couldn't celebrate the impossible difficulty of the job without declaring public school teachers in reality to be such *losers*.

There's cultural and political work to be done, no doubt. But there's also narrative work. We should make the story about teaching worthy of the impact it has on real lives. What the job sounds like should appeal to the best young minds considering their options. One of the purposes of this book is to reinforce the nobility of the profession to bright young people. You really can make it a work of art. Here are some traits I would put at the heart of any job overview for teachers:

Openness: to children, to new ideas, to experiences, to the unknown. We need people who don't wait to try things until they know for sure how they'll turn out. Why? Because the world coming at our students is wildly unpredictable and requires *them* to step into unknowns. Why? Because everybody's life is always a stepping out into unknowns.

Why? Because creativity is always uncertain. It's always an attempt to do what hasn't yet quite been done. When I moved to New York to help start a new school, we did everything without precedents and protocols. But my colleagues were remarkably willing to try things. Could we somehow make caves in our room that you could enter with flashlights to see cave art? Let's try it. Could we turn all this work we've been doing into an evening of sharing with parents? Let's figure it out. Organizers of the City Term program in New York, which centers the entire experience of school on being out in New York City, talk about cultivating "availability" in students. It's an openness to being shaped by new experiences rather than trying first to categorize and tame them. Teachers open themselves up to what's going on in the room too. A colleague told me about the first day of school with his current ninth-graders. He saw a student with an interesting key chain on the table in front of her. He asked her about it, and she talked, and then he decided to ask the other students to take out their keychains and tell the story of them. He said it was a great first day, and he hadn't scripted it at all—but he was open to the idea when it presented itself.

Ingenuity: If you want to see how a teacher really views her job, watch her when the kids don't respond the way she planned. Ingenuity is our reaction to the daily unpredictability of the work—and of our students. It's the audible the teacher calls between classes when the first one doesn't go well. It's the improvised plan on a field trip when the museum doesn't have you on its list. It's the tact and skill that handles an unexpected, inappropriate comment from a student in front of the class. It's also the cleverness to squeeze more out of an experience than the rest of us imagined possible. My colleague Jordan was good at adding layers around whatever city experiences we planned. Once, we were going to take a group of students to see a Eugene O'Neill play. He ran a book group for several weeks after school, discussing the work. He brought the director in to speak with the kids beforehand. Another time, he invited a guest speaker in to talk about immigration and then organized a performance of nineteenth century Irish songs to frame the event. Once, we took students to Brooklyn by walking across the Brooklyn Bridge, and when we gathered for lunch in the Brooklyn Bridge Park, another colleague had kids read aloud parts of Walt Whitman's "Crossing Brooklyn Ferry."

Ingenuity can also involve a capacity to teach through indirection. In the movie *Searching for Bobby Fischer*, a chess teacher played by Ben Kingsley begins his long instruction of a chess prodigy by playing the game Clue with him, by building towers out of chess pieces, and by throwing a ball around a bedroom. At one point, at the chessboard now, he knocks all the pieces away and has his pupil study the empty board. And is there a more famous example of the ingenious teacher using indirection than Mr. Miyagi in *The Karate Kid*, who makes his young charge an effective fighter by requiring him to paint and wax and sand the floor? This seeing of other things we might do because of what we were already planning to do, this capacity to improvise when things don't go as planned, this ability to build understanding indirectly, are all forms of savvy intelligence, of ingenuity.

William James made the claim even stronger: "To know psychology, therefore, is absolutely no guarantee that we shall be good teachers. To advance to that result, we must have an additional endowment altogether, a happy tact and ingenuity to tell us what definite things to say and do when the pupil is before us. That ingenuity in meeting and pursuing the pupil, that tact for the concrete situation, though they be the alpha and omega of the teacher's art, are things to which psychology cannot help us in the least."

Fertility: My mastery of the material I was teaching my first year was solid and real, but it wasn't alive. It wasn't coming from inside me. *I* was studying, as it were, for the test of running a new lesson every day. Ideally, teachers are saturated in what they teach and go on reading and learning and filling their own reservoir of understanding—for the sheer sake of understanding. That ongoing project overflows to students. Tending to the growth of your own mind isn't incidental to teaching. If your own reservoir isn't full, nothing will overflow. I have a colleague who, no matter what unit you're considering or project you're assembling can recommend robust lists of texts you might use with students. Everybody consults him. His mind is full. When a challenge or a circumstance touches it, a flourish of associations is released.

Whimsy: "I would write on the lintels of the door-post, *Whim*," wrote Emerson. "I hope it is somewhat better than whim at last, but we cannot spend the day in explanation." Two of my colleagues in North Carolina had classrooms at opposite ends of a long corridor. Every so often, they Skyped into each other's class and acted like this was matter of fact. With his face on the classroom screen like a domesticated Oz, one would say, hey, Mr. Risko, I wanted to let Zack know that I think he left his pen in my class. Everyone would turn and smile at Zack. Zack would smile. Mr. Risko played it straight and thanked his colleague for checking in. Anything else? No, that's it, his colleague said. I just wanted you to know that Zack left his pen. Then Mr. Risko would sign out, and the Oz-like figure vanished. Those same two teachers played guitar, and on club days they would stand in the hall as school let out, playing simple tunes and making up lyrics about whatever kid happened by: "There goes Kendall, kind of leaning today./I bet he wished all that work would go away./He's got big backpack blues…" Another colleague used to print across the top of assessments: *This Test Is Sponsored by Bob Vila*. I had a colleague in New York who would hand papers back by spinning them like pinwheels on the tables in front of the students. Another colleague put images of historical figures in the top corner of test papers, with thought-bubble quotations urging students on. Why? To break things up. To be unpredictable. To play. There is a line to be honored, for sure, between whimsy and frivolity—which doesn't mean we should be afraid of the line between whimsy and frivolity. But we cannot spend the day in explanation.

One of my very favorite books about teaching is a memoir: *Teacher: The One Who Made the Difference* by Mark Edmundson. The teacher in question, Frank Lears, was formidable, quirky, smart, and a presence unlike anything Edmundson had ever experienced. One winter day, Lears led his class of seniors outside and, to their astonishment, bent over, formed a snowball, and chucked it at one of the boys. (I don't recommend *that*.) A snowball fight ensued that, according to Edmundson, was not only whimsical but transformational: "In ten minutes it is over and Lears and all of us are bending over panting, panting and laughing. It's the first time in a long time at school that I've had something that you could call fun, the first time I've laughed this hard without someone being humiliated. Does Lears see how much he's triumphed today?" A difficult teacher became available to his difficult students. He let his guard down—strategically. This can backfire—horribly. I've seen too many young teachers try too hard to get students to like them. That should be avoided at all costs. Teachers are mentors, not peers. Whimsy has the spirit of the students in mind, but it isn't a workaround for getting them to like you.

We should all shadow a student around school for a day, do everything they do, follow every rule, take all the notes. Colleagues who have done that shake their head. All of them say it's exhausting, and that you spend most of your day sitting down. While whimsy is not the cornerstone of instruction—and the two teachers I cited as my most important exhibited almost none—it does its small part to make students like being at school, and it embodies some of the unpredictability of life in a classroom. Maybe more importantly, to me, pockets of lightness can help teachers stay sane. I used to tell members of my team: the kids you have now need you, but so do the kids you'll teach in ten and twenty years. You owe it to them to pace yourself. You owe it to them not to burn out. Whimsy can be a habit for that long game.

Noticing: Henry James' advice to writers is good for teachers too: "Try to be one of those on whom nothing is lost." So many things require the teacher's attention at once. Especially in your early years, just managing the class through a lesson and avoiding fiasco is a kind of success. But the art of teaching involves watching everything at once and seeing, like 3D-goggled heat, openings and opportunities and problems and needs. Noticing and knowing your students is where the real magic happens. It's what my friend did with his tenth-grader, naming something about the kid that set him on a path that ended up in Mongolia. It's what Ms. Acuff did for me, noticing what I was responding to and offering me next things. It's what Mark Edmundson's teacher did for him toward the end of his high school career as well. A guest speaker in their class talked about Malcolm X, and it jostled the students. Something affected Edmundson too, and his teacher paid attention: "On the way out the door, Lears stopped me. 'You know,' he said, 'I think you might want to look at Malcolm X's autobiography. I think that you would get a lot out of that book." Edmundson's commentary on this simple gesture is moving: "This took me by surprise, this business about myself. Because though Lears was consistently benevolent, there was a kind of gently programmatic quality to his attitude. For quite some time it wasn't clear that he really went a long way in distinguishing us from one another. Who we were and who we might become was our business. He'd give us the necessary goad, send us flying, or dragging, out of the gate, but where we headed was our own concern. But clearly he had some notion of who I was and what I might need. And it touched me greatly, this observation. It reminded me of my father saying that there was something coming up on Carson that I was bound to like. That someone viewed me as more than a shirt and shoes, a walking destination for TV shows and Wonder Bread—this was a singular thing."

As anybody who's had a moment like this knows, this is the greatest gift teachers give their students: knowing them, noticing them, recognizing who they are maybe even before the student herself does, and then offering possibilities—openings—so the student can keep going. "Do you see yonder wicket-gate?" the hero's guide asks at the beginning of John Bunyan's 17th century allegory *A Pilgrim's Progress*. "No," the hero says. His guide tries again. "Then do you see yonder light?" "I think I do," the hero responds. "Then walk toward that light." Students will forever find their own gates; that's just how it works. And teachers forever point toward light that will give them access and options.

Wisdom: A dozen times a day, teachers have to make judgment calls about scenarios they haven't specifically been prepared for. How do you equip people to know what to do before you know what they'll have to do? The best teachers notice all the time, but then they have instincts for what to do to shape or push or encourage or challenge what they notice. That takes wisdom. It takes wisdom to know what a parent is really anxious about or complaining about. It takes wisdom to know when a younger colleague needs to be pushed or instructed, or just given company. It takes wisdom to discern when a student's behavior has nothing really to do with what's going on in your class, but something else, and something larger. It takes wisdom to know when that moment of whimsy is the right call—or the moment of gravity is what students need. You can't easily run professional development training on how to do this. But you can cultivate an atmosphere that values it mightily and honors the way teachers have to exercise judgment more than they have to follow a script. Naming it and celebrating it also reminds teachers as well that their job is to help their students gain wisdom, and not just knowledge.

Feeling. One of my favorite professional development moments involved author and school counselor Michael Thompson speaking to a mixed audience of parents and teachers. He was talking about issues facing adolescent boys. A mother in the crowd told him she was worried because her son wouldn't ever cry, in fact fought hard against it if he was clearly starting to. She said she told him over and over it was okay, that men and boys can cry, that that doesn't mean they're weak, but he wouldn't listen, and what could she do? She was clearly distressed, and when she finished, Michael Thompson said, Can I ask you a question? Do you think your son has ever seen his father cry? The woman lowered her head and said no. Michael Thompson went on: Has he seen an uncle cry, do you think? Or a neighbor? Or any adult male in his life? The woman holding the microphone didn't answer because she was sobbing.

To teach students without ever addressing the emotional part of life is negligence. To teach as if the entire enterprise of what we do is intellectual and rational is arrogance. To pay attention to emotions without exhibiting emotions ourselves is confusing. It's a lot of work to manage a classroom of students, and sometimes stiffness and order are the right strategy. But over time, if teachers want to incite life in students, they have to straddle the line of maintaining the right distance from them and embodying the kind of fullness they want their students to embrace. You can't tell a kid it's okay to cry if you never cry yourself.

A documentary about a Japanese teacher called *Children Full of Life* makes this case in a compelling way. In the film, a fourth-grade teacher, who announces to his students on day one that the class goal for the year is understanding how to be happy, uses writing exercises to cultivate empathy and community. In one heartbreaking instance, a young student describing the death of his grandmother leads to another student breaking down, recalling the death of her father. Any teacher who watches will probably feel ambivalent: this teacher has created a risky scenario. But he's far enough along in his relationship with them, and he's established the conditions in which the engagement of their emotions could become a beautiful thing. The boldness of making emotional experiences the explicit aim of classwork is enviable. And why shouldn't they be, if emotions are the heart of our most meaningful experiences?

Obviously, teachers need to be poised in their classrooms and not wear their hearts on their sleeves, in the same way that parents don't share their entire emotional life with their children. That's not what kids need. And sometimes when a student's own emotional life is volatile, she needs a counselor not the teacher. But we are emotional beings nonetheless, children and adults, and as Parker Palmer wrote, we teach who we are. The line we straddle is to always teach to what our students need from us—not what we need from them.

Joy: One of my colleagues one time, frustrated by the usual politics and wrangling of a large organization, burst out in a meeting with this declaration: I just want our kids to like school! We teachers have to like it first. It still seems to me you can't have a great school if teachers don't want to come to work every day—and don't like the other teachers they're working with. I don't mean by joy false cheerfulness. I mean a deep sense that what we're doing is vital and that for all the headaches and slights of the job it is one in which we get to be fully human and fully authentic—and it gives something back to us too. This is hard to sustain on your own. The best formula, I think, for maintaining joy is to put people in good teams that support each other and draw out each other's creativity and personality. School leaders have to model this too. My own boss is an exceptional leader, able to manage a very complex organization in a way that impresses everyone—including me. I've watched him for a while now, and for all his efficiencies and for all his institutional savvy, the thing I notice is that when he walks around greeting teachers and having brief conversations with them, he always manages to smile and usually at some point laughs at something. He's the best listener I've ever worked for; sitting across from him you feel you have his full attention. But I suspect it's the habitual ability to smile and laugh—maybe because he's so efficient otherwise—that makes him a leader and not just an administrator. He leads with joy.

Openness. Ingenuity. Fertility. Whimsy. Noticing. Wisdom. Feeling. Joy. These aren't just traits we *need* but privileges we get to exercise: Here is a job that allows you to embody virtues like these. Here is a job that needs you to be a full human being. To have work that focuses on at least these traits is a good way to be in the world. If this is the job profile, at heart, you really do get to teach life, and dwell in it as you do.

And it's fair to ask how you can scale teaching virtues like this. I won't pretend you can. There are things that just refuse to be scaled. Fire, for example. Which doesn't mean you can't light things from fire, over and over and over, and create a thousand versions of that original fire in a thousand separate flames.

LESSON 18

GROUNDHOG YEARS

*In any classroom, something is always happening. They
keep you on your toes. They keep you fresh. You'll never
grow old, but the danger is you might have the mind of an
adolescent forever.*

—— Frank McCourt, *Teacher Man*

Every teacher experiences time in an unsettling way. We talk
about it too. When new students show up in the autumn, it's
forever the same age parading down the hall, while at the
same time, as they arrive, you've aged one more year. It's a
strange way to register time, as if only you and your
colleagues are handing back years, and the kids inhabit
Neverland. And I'm twenty-five years too late with this
thought, but I would have liked to have taken a picture of
myself on day one of every school year, preferably in the
same spot and in the same pose—and then taken pictures of
every new group of students I received. I'm imagining a kind
of time lapse or flip book of myself ageing, while the students
go on being suspended variations of young adolescence.

I love school for the way community forms around quest.
You're trying to do something interesting and important and
life forming, and through the trial-and-error of that collective
effort, deep bonds form: between students and faculty,
between students and students, between faculty and faculty.

It's not sacred exactly because there's no appeal to something outside of each other to give the work meaning. But it's almost sacred, partly because kids are involved, and the lives of all kids are poignant with possibility and pain, partly because every teacher worth her salt gives her heart to the job. My former colleague Carole, on days when we would have writing conferences with the entire class, said it felt like giving a pint of blood to every kid.

I love school for the density of community that can be created, but I love school too for the way it reveals the passage of experience to you over and over. What other job has such a close relationship to—I'm tempted to capitalize it—time? What other job, outside of religious communities, feels like it follows a liturgical year? When I think back on my job in North Carolina, I still see each year pegged by cycling projects and activities, and I associate them all with weather and light and mood: the Year 1000 Festival in early October, when the morning air as we set up had a bite but wasn't yet too cold to be out in (the autumn wind occasionally blowing over tri-folds on our marketplace tables). Then short documentary films we made about medieval journeys that connected various cultures around the globe. We'd organize and do any filming outdoors before Thanksgiving, then we'd come back and edit and present before the long winter break. In the middle of that would be Veterans Day, when as a middle school we invited fifteen or so area veterans and set them up in rooms for students to rotate through; and somewhere in there the National Geographic Geography Bee in front of the whole middle school. To break things up one year, two teachers dressed as secret service agents brought in the question booklet in a handcuffed briefcase.

The toughest stretch of any school year is the period between New Year's and Spring Break. Even in North Carolina, the days were cold, the light was stingy, illnesses got passed around. And I always got sick at least once every year, usually then, usually flu. The two worst parts of the job:

Sisyphean grading, and relentless kid germs. I see my students in that stretch, working on their longest, most demanding essay of the year. I see one of my best students ever write a long, elegant essay that ignored the prompt entirely and threw me into a quandary. (I ended up giving him high praise for the paper he'd written—then asking him to write another.) I see parent-conferences and basketball games. I see myself staying home sick but coming in late in the day to coach the 8th grade boys' basketball game, then getting questioned by the head of school for setting a bad example—missing class but showing up for sports. Coaching with a fever once, I cursed at a kid for not guarding his man. Absolutely should have stayed home in bed. At a parent conference once, mid-winter, my phone rings, and it's my wife, and I know she wouldn't interrupt unless it was an emergency, because she knows what I am doing that day, so I excuse myself and answer, and she's panicking because our two-year-old daughter has somehow locked herself in her room and is crying and what should she do? I see thirty-degree days followed by sixty-degree days, then thirty-degree days again. I see myself arriving at school in the dark and driving home in the dark. I see our faculty gathered in a room after school to get the news about raises for the following year, just before contracts go out, and people leaving and shaking their heads, laughing a little (because it is what we expected—cost of living) and trying to cheer each other on. In world-historical terms, a colleague used to say, we're privileged, every one of us, it's good work and rewarding. Still, people would go for a drink after work later to talk about something else, forget about compensation for an hour. Unless you had a game you had to coach. Or you were running the game clock for another coach who had a game. Then maybe you picked up fast food in a drive-through on the way home at night. Read to your kids if you made it before their bedtime. Read a little yourself before yours. Avoided grading if you could. When I was young, in winter, I used to go outside and start the car for my mother so the windshield would defrost and the car would be warm for when she came out to drive us to school. Sitting in my Subaru in North Carolina in the driveway, waiting for the frost on the windshield to crack and calf, I think of that. There were no real holidays in February. School didn't let out for Valentine's Day. You held on for March, for Spring Break, when, in North Carolina at least, the weather helped you feel different, and basketball season ended, and we got grades and comments in, and, after a few faculty work days, had a real break, two weekends and one week: ten days to sleep later and go slower and read and wonder again in your leisure if you'd made the right choice, about teaching, about North Carolina, about everything.

And then the light returns. Not solstice light—equinox. And after Spring Break, you see the end, and you can rally the kids to anything again. We did our best work in April and May, preparing kids for what we called The Great Debate: formal, structured, one-on-one debates, with high-school-kid coaches and outside judges, and cameras to stream the debates live for parents to watch on their computers. And you'd drive into school, and it was light out, and when you left school at 4:30 or 5:00, still light. And year-end events began to offer their relief, their adrenaline, and their melancholy. We saved our overnight field trip for the last month of school. We used to ponder moving it to the beginning of the year to build community, but we liked it at the end to mark instead what we'd been through. We'd go to a YMCA camp in the mountains. Kids hiked and did ropes courses, analyzed ponds and streams, learned about mountain wildlife. We roasted marshmallows over a big outdoor fire, and when it got too dark to see, we'd hike back up to the lodge-like residence, and after the students were checked into their rooms, the faculty would sit out on the porch. Away from city lights, you could see the Milky Way. And we'd talk about the year. But I always loved an earlier hour, right after afternoon activities were over when we'd gather as a grade on the big lodge porch and we'd talk to them briefly then take a class picture. Before dinner, students would hang out there, and when teachers drifted around talking to them, it was different. It was like the supervision was over (it wasn't), and we enjoyed their company and played little games like this: who in the class is most like what Ms. White would have been like in 7th grade? Or Mr. Risko? Or maybe we'd talk about the year behind us, or 8th grade ahead. Always the same, though, for us teachers: the kids every time were exactly this age and exactly in this place, and we knew what to expect, we knew who they were. We'd seen them before, in other faces. We'd taught them in the guise of older siblings, older students. And we kept getting older and gathering on the YMCA porch to admire the view and confess fatigue and celebrate success and then wonder, every time, if we might change the trip next year, just to mix things up, just to keep ourselves fresh. But we didn't. And I loved that trip and loved that job. The predictability, the cycle of time, was strange and vivid and comforting too. But it was one of the reasons I decided finally to leave, to try a new challenge, because I wasn't convinced comfort was a good enough aim for my life.

My friend Dave is still there. He's one of the best teachers I've ever known. We are exactly the same age. I taught 7th grade history; he taught 8th. My students would become his students. We coached basketball together. The year his son was born, I covered his coaching duties for several weeks, and he wanted to pay me for it out of the stipend he received, but I wouldn't take it, so instead he bought two tickets and drove us to see Bob Dylan in Winston Salem. My father had loved Dylan, but Dave was a true devotee—a Dylan head. He had boxes and boxes filled with bootleg CD's. He burned dozens of shows for me, spanning Dylan's career. Dave knew seemingly everything there was to know about Dylan's so-called Never Ending Tour, and after that night in Winston-Salem, we joined Dylan's wanderings as we could. The very next weekend we traveled to Augusta, Georgia for a show. After that, we went to see Dylan anytime he came within a five-hour drive of Raleigh. Part of measuring out those years. When is Dylan coming through? I think together we saw 15 to 20 shows. Dave would know exactly. Like his teaching routines, his memory was methodical and seemingly infallible. If Dylan played an obscure song, Dave would smile and tell me later that he hadn't played that since 1998, or whenever it was, that he'd only played it three times total on the famous decades-spanning tour. Dave was the most reliable person I've ever met—mentally, morally, professionally. For as long as I knew him, he had a syllabus for his classes that mapped out the year entirely. He tweaks and improves it, and is dynamic and imaginative, but his system is in place too—he hasn't changed classrooms in nineteen years—I imagine he will probably retire there. And I loved teaching with Dave, and I might have happily gone on handing students off to him to retirement, but then I left after year fourteen.

No school year goes by that I don't look over my shoulder and think I could have been happy staying in North Carolina forever: Y1K, documentary films, a difficult essay, The Great Debate, the porch at the YMCA retreat, the first day of school, standing in the hall, surveying the new crowd, going once or twice a year to catch Dylan with Dave, breaking down the show and the set list on the long ride home at night from Charlotte or Columbia or Washington or wherever. But I left. I didn't want Time to have the full upper hand, lulling me where it, and not I, wanted to go. I wanted a lot of things, I know; they contradicted. I left. And because he stayed put and will likely go on staying put, Dave will know things that I don't know. Beautiful things. He will glimpse things because he abides there. And I will know different things, beautiful things too, because I wandered.

ON-THE-JOB POLITICS

To create in a person the ability to look at the world for himself, to make his own decisions…. To ask questions of the universe, and then learn to live with those questions.

— James Baldwin, "A Talk to Teachers"

A big part of me wants to leave politics out by the curb, invite us all into a purer space where the interactions between students and teachers are compassionate, challenging, life-giving, and controversy-free. Because we deal with young people, we teachers might be forgiven for wanting to protect them from conflicts the grown-ups clearly can't master. Part of me wants to do that. Part of me wants to say even to high school students, you'll get the politics head-on soon enough. It comes with the orientation packet in college. When you're old enough to vote, that's a good age to start arguing through the issues. For now, take advantage of the chance to think about things you won't have time to ponder when you're older and making a living and raising a family—and arguing politics. For now, learn how the natural world works and how our understanding of nature has changed drastically over time, read stories about the past and the present, about how people lived, as many different people as you can in as many different contexts, learn how they organized themselves, what they valued and loved and feared and fought about, how they mistreated each other and how they made peace, learn how to work with other people on a task, practice being creative, practice listening a lot, take up an instrument, try a lot of things and don't worry that you abandon almost all of them, speak in front of groups, learn another language, learn two, including the language of math, read a lot of poetry, read a lot of everything, go out into your community and do something helpful and compassionate, learn about yourself and who you want to be, make some friends, practice apologizing.

Part of me thinks we push kids too fast into controversial things, and part of me thinks that's a reflection of our own insecurities and needs. Having gone through our own processes and reached hard-won conclusions, we're eager to hasten students to those same resolutions—to save them and spare them the blind spots we ourselves overcame with great difficulty. That's not the worst thing in the world. But to teach the Holocaust in sixth grade, or imperialism in seventh, or systemic racism in eighth grade or tenth requires deftness and wisdom—not just good intentions. Maybe that goes without saying. But maybe teachers who have made a dozen passes themselves through an issue or topic might need to self-consciously work back to what a first pass should feel like. Otherwise we coach from the finish line with bullhorn clarity and teach what to think rather than how to approach thinking. It may feel good to us without being good for students where they are. Maybe here stories are still the best entry points. Maybe Anne Frank's diary is exactly the right way for young people to learn about the Holocaust for the first time. Maybe Laurie Halse Anderson's historical novel *Chains* is the perfect way for a sixth-grader to start thinking about the complex racial and political history of America. Part of me thinks there's no reason to be squeamish at all about politics as politics. It's a necessary and even exciting aspect of the world, an arena for idealism and heroism as well as power and privilege, and there's no age too young to explore that collective space. The challenge is only to make it age appropriate.

But then part of me thinks we should let students enjoy what Erik Erikson called a "moratorium," an insulated stretch of life in which you can figure out who you are and what you want before you take on your own struggle in the world, whether for money, meaning, or some larger cause. Part of me thinks we should focus on building capacities in students to think and feel with range and depth. We should think of education as a fairly constant switching of lenses so that students become agile thinkers, capable of a thousand flourishing options: building companies or products, serving in the Peace Corps, serving in the Coast Guard, designing new things, making things with your hands, cooking for other people, sitting in a lab developing new vaccines for new virus variants, writing poetry or code, nursing the sick and researching cures, practicing law, fighting injustice, building buildings, serving in government, serving in law enforcement, acting or dancing or painting, or even maybe, who knows, teaching. And while we're at it: learning what it means to be good parents and partners and friends and citizens, and being interesting human beings who get along with themselves and have interesting projects.

Part of me thinks that's what we should do: help students figure out what it means to flourish before they contend. But part of me knows that's the danger of my own perspective, my Romanticism for sure, but also my own experiences, and that if I'm not careful I can imagine school as an unspoiled island, like the one in Shakespeare's *Tempest*, and be too taken with the innocent Miranda declaring a brave new world to pay attention to chained Caliban on the other side of the story. The limitation of my Romanticism is that my circumstances have allowed it and nourished it, and it is a luxury not every young person can assume. I pay attention to all that too. I grew up with certain advantages and certain struggles. We were middle class until my parents divorced, and then we lived at the border of being almost poor. My father told my mother she could get us qualified for reduced lunch tickets at school, but she refused because she saw it as a stigma, refused to think we were poor, though she made a little more than minimum wage, skipped meals herself so we could eat the whole box of Tuna Helper or Hamburger Helper, four growing boys with an unpredictable father, but a father who read books and gave me an ambition to outread him. And I was white, and I was male, though when I was in school we didn't name race or gender much yet, and we didn't use the language of privilege. There was indeed a trail I could follow to get where I wanted to get, but it wasn't well blazed or, where I lived, very crowded, and, for me, it was full of financial and emotional obstacles, but there was a path there regardless. I took it. It was what I could see to do. I understand now that even what felt to me like my own determined work was an option unavailable in the same way to others. I see that in a way I wouldn't have at the time. And I understand how someone arguing that the best education holds off conclusions and positions and teaches students to argue and think and narrate from as many points of view as possible can reinforce keeping things just the way they are— that it's the people with the most security who can afford to suspend judgment or celebrate negative capability. What looks to one person like patience registers to someone else as indifference. And yet still, in the end, we can't do the thinking work for our students; we have to create the conditions in which they think and grow themselves. I would consider it a sign of failure if my students didn't move on from me and end up holding different beliefs, different loves, different convictions. How to balance these things wisely is not obvious. If it were, we'd all be doing it better.

My school in New York City was in a sober, peculiar space the day after the 2016 election. The atmosphere was less shock than grief. Our school was called out in the *New York Post* for circulating an email about supporting each other in the wake of the Trump victory, as if a natural disaster had occurred. And just to be clear, I was in plenty of shock too. As the early returns stumbled in, from my New York bubble I kept telling my pessimistic partner that Hillary was in good shape; she was going to win. It might be tighter than expected, I acknowledged, but she would win. And yet at school the next day I felt unsure about how we were handling the results and our reactions with the students. There was a collective faculty daze that we didn't hold back from the kids. People gathered soberly around a laptop in the cafeteria to watch Hillary's concession speech. I did too. But I wondered if we should have held our collective reaction back for afterwards, should have aimed for more neutrality if we could. We probably should have tried harder to ask what our students needed from us, not what we needed in that moment. Hindsight being 20-20.

We see from our own height (Wittgenstein). We teach who we are (Parker Palmer). I know that part of why I'm allergic to crowding young minds with politics and controversies is because my own father crowded mine too young. The year my father moved across town to a two-bedroom townhouse, he started reading Ayn Rand and became an avid, vocal libertarian. I was thirteen at the time, and he didn't think that was too young to examine the injustices of taxation or to understand the ideology of Soviet communism. My father was a man without the audience he craved. He wasn't doing what he wanted to be doing. He wasn't living where he wanted to be living. For several years—my early teen-age years—we drove to the mall every Tuesday night, and he would stand in the B. Dalton bookstore reading while my brothers and I roamed the stores and corridors, each with a dollar to spend. When I went back to the bookstore, my father would be standing by the small shelf of philosophy books, surrounded by the much larger section of Bibles and Bible-reading aids, and he would have the arm of his glasses in his mouth as he stood reading, and when he saw me, he'd say, here, son, I marked something for you, I want you to read something. And he'd hand me a book about economics or religion or political philosophy, and he'd wait for me to respond with admiration or outrage. In the car, he lectured us on politics, usually in a tone of complaint. In a snowstorm once, he defied the mayor's request that everyone stay inside, and he took us out in his Chevrolet because he had a right to, he thought, and also to impress his young girlfriend by braving the unplowed streets. Because of his libertarianism, I attended a meeting of the Ayn Rand Society my first year in college. An upperclassman approached me casually and asked how I'd become a "Randian." (I didn't go back again.) Eventually, my father pivoted hard to the left. An avowed socialist, he championed Castro and Che Guevara, even Mao and Lenin. When I moved to London after college, he sent me pictures of himself wearing T-shirts protesting the Gulf War, and one showing a map of the U.S. with *Indian Territory* written across it. And I reacted against his activism and certainty. Not quite politically conservative, I leaned traditional in my tastes. One of my fellow students in high school said I reminded her of Alex Keaton on "Family Ties," which made me start watching that show. While my father let his hair grow long, I wore the era's safe button-downs and khakis. I converted to an evangelical version of Christianity. When my thinking made its journey toward more liberal commitments, it was different from my father's in tone and style and nuance and intensity.

I bring all this baggage with me to the job, and I try my best to check it at the door, or to be aware of it all the time. I recognize it for sure whenever elections roll around, and my colleagues and I set up a unit of instruction, or when we're figuring out what to do for Black History Month, or Veterans Day, or we're designing simulations or debates engaging current events, or figuring out the learning part of service learning initiatives, or debating whether a reading list is representative enough, or too Western and white. How to teach topics and texts that are unavoidably saturated in politics without making the instruction itself political, without taking political sides?

When I started teaching, the rebuke to my anxiety about politics came straight from John Dewey. Schools, he said, are laboratories of democracy. We are preparing students both for life and for citizenship. Our work isn't separate from politics; it is preparation for it. That used to seem to me to put the classroom focus on how democracy works and why it's preferable to the alternatives ("the worst form of government," as Churchill quipped, "except for all the others"). The boundary of all our instruction was democracy itself: while people disagreed about policies and perspectives, all of us could agree on the framework for debate and political competition, and we could work in schools to understand it better.

That sounds way too easy now, even if it mostly still sounds right. A lot has happened since Dewey celebrated democracy. He was writing before Brown v. Board of Education, for starters. Schools should articulate and account for as much as they can of history's problems and corrections. It's a different kind of question, though, to ask ourselves as teachers how to advance the ongoing dynamic of social change—of politics—*inside* school. A teacher with a roomful of students who identify as Democrats (or Republicans) but for a single Republican (or Democrat) has an obligation not to make the outlier feel the instruction is stacked against him. This has been especially hard in recent years, as the well-known polarization of the country has gone on deepening. But if the conservative teacher in Alabama (or New York) mustn't mock the Democratic candidate, the progressive teacher in Manhattan (or Montgomery) must return the favor of neutrality—inside school.

At my New York school we have something we call the World Course. It's an interdisciplinary idea that weaves through the larger curriculum, and its focus is on global understanding. We want students to leave us ready to engage the rapidly changing world. We're a young school, and the curriculum remains a work in progress, but at some point in our third year we realized we were in danger of making the world in our World Course seem primarily to be a set of problems to be solved (climate change), issues to be engaged (income inequality), injustices to be corrected (racism). The world obviously is all those things, but is it only those things? Isn't it also where we pursue our passions, make friends, struggle with and still love our families and our cities, experience beauty and joy, disappointment and grief, patriotic pride and national disappointment? Isn't it also where we make meaning before we die? A big part of education should be understanding the many contexts inside which all that life happens: the cultural contexts around us, the historical contexts behind us, the biographical contexts inside us. And where certain people have advantages and certain others deep disadvantages, understanding those imbalances is central to education. And where the problems are systems and structures and not simply bad individual actors, we need to uncover and expose and set our students up to be agents of change and improvement. And where basic conditions of access to food and health and safety aren't present, not much else matters until they are. And *that* political issue is larger than schools.

I used to have a friendly debate with one of my World Course colleagues. He said we would be successful if every kid we graduated went into the Peace Corps. I asked him what the world would be without poetry or art, or people sitting in labs researching medical cures, or even entrepreneurs financing water treatment facilities in developing countries. Or people making movies. Or editing books. Didn't we want to educate good people who would work in banks and in government too? He shrugged. I want to fill the Peace Corps, he said. Anyone could see that we were both idealizing our sense of the world, and our own experience of it. What did his father teach or argue that made it likely he'd think like he did, that led him eventually to serve, as he did, in the Peace Corps? I had a religious period, tried and failed to write a novel. All of that is somehow wrapped up in how I am in a classroom. It's part of what I bring to students because it's part of what I am.

I'm not sure how exactly we should move forward as a society. No teacher is. It seems to be getting harder to talk with each other about complicated, controversial things. As I finish this brief meditation, saturated as it is with limits and flaws, the election of 2020 is freshly behind us, and the Covid-19 pandemic is still ravaging. Our racial reckoning continues. I do not know how we repair ourselves and figure out the best, healthy, just, flourishing way forward. I'm committed to being in the conversation. And willing to be proved wrong. I was reared also not to lose arguments; that's in me too, and I try to check that every day. And what do you, generous reader, carry into the conversation with you? For all these qualifications, I'm still not sure at what age and how much students need to internalize particular political ambiguities. It's timing and touch, as well as convictions and ideas. I think. And humble listening, deep, humble listening, that's also somehow not afraid.

DIGITAL DIETS

*Inevitably, the year before you were born looks like Eden,
and the year after your children were born looks like
Mad Max.*

— Alison Gopnik, *The Gardener and the Carpenter*

In my first teaching job in 1996, two walls of my classroom
were filled with old chalkboards. I wrote notes with real
chalk. I think, but can't even remember for sure, that I had a
television on a cart with a VCR in that room. Although
maybe I had to sign it out from the library. The same year I
was hired, the school brought in its first technology
instructor, and he set up a lab of desktops that the middle
school students I taught would rotate through once a week. I
was young and in the mood for innovation, and so I tried to
coordinate with my colleague as I could. We began where you
began in those days after some keyboarding practice: we did
PowerPoint slideshows on some historical topic. Cutting edge
stuff. Sitting next to me as students delivered their maiden
presentations, the headmaster leaned over and smiled: "A lot
of effort," he remarked, "went into the sizzle of effects; not
as much into the content." He was a little too pleased with
this observation, but he was right.

My second school was founded by two software
entrepreneurs who donated land at the edge of their

sprawling company campus in North Carolina as a kind of lab school for using technology. When we opened, every classroom had a line of Dell Desktops around three walls—one per student. Every room had its own printer. The "white boards" we wrote on with markers were slate-gray to look like chalkboards. Students convinced me to use the search engine Dogpile, though you still spotted people Asking Jeeves. The data projectors warmed up like old console TVs. Distribution lists in our email revolutionized school communication. Learning a bit of HTML, we built our own web pages for our classes. Heady days.

After a few years, we transitioned to laptops, one per student. In my fourth year, I think, I learned how to edit video using Adobe Premiere software and got interested in different ways of using video in my classroom but also in the life of the school. I started doing a video yearbook for the 7th grade class, shooting footage of everything we did, organizing the tapes, then devoting eighty to a hundred hours of my final weeks of school to compiling a one-hour film, complete with soundtrack.

In 2016, students at my school in New York used MacBook Airs for everything. They had access to iPads. Every classroom had data projectors and smart boards. Our halls were filled with video screens on which teachers could project student work, or the school could rotate announcements and images of its Instagram page. When you entered the building and approached the main staircase, you were confronted with a wall of nine screens that offered separate images of school activities or world news feeds—or a single joined image. Students surreptitiously checked their iPhones. They weren't supposed to. Smart watches fed texts as gently as a touch on a sleeve. We interviewed long-distance candidates via FaceTime and Zoom. This past year when Covid hit, we all moved school itself to our various screens.

When I started teaching, we were trying to figure out ways to use the new technologies. Now, one of the tasks is to figure out ways to contain and limit the digital flow. One of my colleagues threatened to take a picture of his belly button and make it the screen saver on all his devices to dramatize our navel-gazing devotion. Is there an app for that? Recently, when we developed an innovative band of writing in our middle school and high school, we decided to have students use notebooks and pens, partly just to slow them down and reduce the rippling distractions of the digital world. Left to their own devices, they plug in ear buds to listen to music while they work. I tell them, we might be wrong; you really might think better with music, we don't know. But have you really tried the opposite? I tell them, I know, your teachers work with ear buds in as well. This may just be our world. I may be shouting at the ocean to go shape a different shore.

Something comes up in a class: How old *was* Fitzgerald when he wrote *The Great Gatsby*? Did Frederick Douglass actually meet Abraham Lincoln? Students don't have to be spurred into action. Faster than a Big Mac being handed across a counter, someone has the answer on a screen. Students working on a task together snap into action and create a Google doc to share. I walk past a table in a common area, and two kids are flying planes in a flight simulator. One kid is playing chess. Another is on Spotify. At least half have ear buds in. Walk into any classroom and stare discreetly over the shoulders of students with laptops: they toggle back and forth between various windows, chatting and checking messages, working on a task for the class they're in, working on a task for a different class, checking teacher web pages, checking on news feeds or social media that's not firewalled by the school.

I'm not qualified to comment on the effects of all this screen time on our brains. But it doesn't take a scientist to see that our attention spans are addled. It's not surprising that mindfulness initiatives have become popular in schools. A few years ago, I started noticing that students, sent off to start a long-term task, were coming to my desk within minutes to say they couldn't find anything on their topic or question. Our laptops are like jars in which mounds of M&Ms surround a few carrot sticks. We place them in front of students and tell them to remember to eat well. That we're asking a lot from young people to ignore all these distractions is clear from the struggles full-grown adults have to manage technology wisely. Two writer friends use the program Freedom to block internet access while they work. If those of us with fully developed brains need external help to resist digital distractions, it can't be enough just to tell kids: don't eat the M&Ms.

In the Bob Dylan biopic *I'm Not There*, a character chides the young Dylan stand-in for singing about Depression-era boxcars when race riots were going on around them. *Live your own time, child*, the character says. *Sing about your own time.* Schools have to live their own time too, which means using and teaching technology. And that's not just a cynical concession. Technology does make things more efficient, and it does open up whole worlds of information. When I was growing up, I walked to the end of the driveway every morning to retrieve our small-town newspaper. At the picnic table we had in our kitchen, I read it with my toast before school. The front section had eight or ten pages. That was my window to what was going on in the world: a few syndicated columns of national news, a lot of local stories, then sports and comics, a breakdown of a Bridge hand, and classified ads. Now, every day I skim and read online versions of *The New York Times*, *The Washington Post*, *The Guardian*, and an aggregate of other news sources from all over the world. I also nervously check news sites when I'm in the middle of a task and want a brain break, or I toggle to them just because they're there, an easy click away—a bowl of candy on a desk.

What I want to say to students: You are all a jumpy generation. It's not your fault. And I know young people aren't as worried about digital overstimulation as we older folks are. I can't believe I'm finally seeing myself as that person, citing generational things. I do watch students navigate what looks like overwhelming distractions and still get good work done. My older daughter used to alarm me by typing texts under the kitchen table without looking at her phone. But she went on to study ancient Greek and is planning on becoming a teacher. She figured out how to navigate the digital storm, as most of her peers have too.

As I said about politics, I'm willing to find out I'm wrong. But I'll offer at least this: access to information is not the same thing as understanding. It's barely an arrow on a sign on the road to real wisdom. Gaining wisdom requires some slowing down, some patient, sustained concentration. We have to slow our minds down. Let things come. We can leap at information; we have to put ourselves in the way of understanding, and wait on it. A century and a half before Google went live, Thoreau saw people all around him addled by the telegraph-swift flow of nineteenth-century news: "Hardly a man takes a half-hour's nap after dinner, but when he wakes he holds up his head, and asks, 'What's the news?' as if the rest of mankind had stood his sentinels."

To young teachers I would say, without reservation, use technology. Use a lot of it. Try all kinds of things. Model for students stepping into the new. But model how to measure out technology use too. Step away from screens. Build islands of non-digital experience into every classroom journey. Screens make us feverish. Freud said that protection against stimulation is as important for the mind as the reception and processing of stimulation. He knew something about an addled generation too. Students pick up the stimulation side of the equation without effort. They need our help balancing that with habits that may look old fashioned.

I led a group of students to the Museum of Modern Art once as part of a weeklong elective. We had one destination:

Van Gogh's "Starry Night." There was no sheet of questions for them to answer. No assignment to sketch anything. We got on the subway then made the trek from there, fought through the crowds of people taking pictures of the painting, crowds like the ones that crush the space around the Mona Lisa, and we just looked at the painting. Took it in. What are we supposed to do? a student asked. Nothing, I said. Look at it, I said. What do we do when we've done that? he asked. I said, look again.

DR. CAPPS

In this world ... you must be oh so smart, or oh so
pleasant. Well, for years I was smart. I recommend
pleasant. You may quote me.

— Jimmy Stewart as Elwood P. Dowd, *Harvey*

Several years ago, when my friend Jeff emailed me to say our
old mentor Dr. Capps had died, we were both a little stunned,
and we swapped tributes through the digital air, and we
started talking about meeting up in Princeton again just to
pay tribute there, where we had known him when we were
seminary students, struggling with how to believe. Both of us
had adored him. Both of us had gone to seminary with great
needs, and we weren't sure how to meet them. Dr. Capps
became a kind of father figure for us, without being really a
guide. We had other guides. Jeff was a Kierkegaard reader; I
was devoted to William James. We had other favorite
professors too—better teachers in front of a room—people
like Diogenes, who I described earlier, with intellectual heft
and charisma to spare. Dr. Capps in the front of the room
was like someone trying not to disturb anything else that
might be going on in people's minds. He spoke like a guest,
not like a host, as if he were grateful for us merely being there
at all. And for all Dr. Capps' meekness, Jeff and I both loved
him more than anyone because he seemed as wounded as we

felt and didn't pretend otherwise and because he set aside theological problems without guilt or regret and because when we went to talk to him outside of class he listened without an agenda and nodded a lot and said to our crazy theories and objections to orthodox beliefs: Boy, that sounds about right, doesn't it? As if he, despite his years and his tenure, suddenly realized he shared our bewilderment.

Once when I told him I was having a hard time getting anything out of church anymore and suggested that services should aim for twenty minutes tops, with some music and some readings and then music to send us on—no sermon— he nodded sympathetically and said, that sounds about right, doesn't it? He had given up feeling pressured by clarity and truth. In his presence, the Christian life seemed like a long convalescence that shouldn't be interrupted. He wanted compassion in the raw. All of us had been hurt, and we should leave the hurt alone, not describe it or redeem it with our various theologies. Sitting in a diner on Witherspoon Street, he listened to Jeff's and my stories of struggle to break free of inherited things. He didn't have advice. He just affirmed that a transition in religious understanding was always hard. He didn't suggest that we needed to figure anything out. And even though, away from the diner, we went on tying ourselves in philosophical knots and engaging in unwinnable debates, we felt better in his company, and we kept seeking him out.

At the time, we were sure we needed answers and strategies. At the time, we assumed those strategies involved thinkers and books. Jeff moved on from Kierkegaard to Foucault. I went from James to Richard Rorty. Both of our fathers had left our families when we were young. Both of us were eager for new mentors. Every Tuesday, Jeff and I went to Burger King after Dr. Capps' class because Tuesday was 99-cent Whopper day on Nassau Street, and, after Whoppers, we'd go to the Small World Café and drink coffee by the front windows, and we'd tell stories about our small-town lives and then square off Rorty against Foucault and brainstorm paths forward that might keep us in Princeton or, if we were lucky, New York. We talked about staying in school. The big questions still preoccupied us. We took them personally. We attended the seminary but dreamed of the university across the street. Both of us thought of applying to do PhDs there. But as our last year approached we decided around the same time that we wouldn't do doctorates. I planned to write a novel. Jeff was going to study to become a massage therapist. I went back South to teach and write. Jeff went home to West Virginia to live slow and build a cabin. Both of us started families, determined to be better fathers than we'd known. Two people who had every reason not to look back, we kept looking back, more interested in redeeming what we'd been than casting it aside and starting again.

I told Dr. Capps one time I was worried about self-indulgence, self-involvement, turning inward so much I wouldn't be able to get out or love anyone or anything in the world. It was the only time he ever corrected me. I just think, he said, you have to be at home inside yourself to be any good to anybody else. In other words, he was saying—or what I heard: I wasn't warped; I was okay. That's all Jeff or I ever wanted from him anyway.

Then Dr. Capps told us a personal story of his own. He was a child, and his older brother kept misbehaving, exasperating his parents, and finally they put him in the car and drove up the hill to an orphanage. They told him he was being so difficult they were going to leave him there for good. In the back seat of the car, Dr. Capps started pleading with his parents on his brother's behalf: *He'll do better, don't do this, he'll be better.* A story that still moves me to recall and that I still remind Jeff about when we talk on the phone and quote Dr. Capps in his trembling hurt voice. His experience of vulnerability was evident in everything he said. And somehow it reassured the vulnerability we felt, made us feel we would be okay.

I praised a different teacher earlier for inciting life inside me, for drawing me outside my own concerns to something greater. What do you *treasure?* Diogenes asked us over and over that first year in seminary. And that made me want to build my life, my sense of things, on something worthy. But Dr. Capps recognized what was going on inside us and was patient with the things holding us back, and that may have mattered more. Maybe all great teaching is a combination of what these two professors embodied: Diogenes' inspiration, pushing us up and out toward something grand and beautiful and inspiring; Dr. Capps' recognition, the teacher getting what a student is about, or trying to be about, and protecting the space around that so it can grow. The writer Philip Roth described his most important college teacher this way: "She valued me. This is what I needed and what I got.... Look, somebody has to tell you that you're smart and that you're doing the right thing."

When I talk about Diogenes, the stories and quotations still flow. I feel honored to have had him as a teacher. He pointed me ahead. But when I talk about seminary with my friend Jeff, it's Dr. Capps we go on missing. We miss him. We loved him. Because he saw our vulnerability—he saw us—and made it all somehow bearable, okay.

LESSON 22

PARENTS

*... she opened the door wide and said, in her indifferent
tone, "Children inside." When one mother tried to lead her
reluctant son into the dark parlor, Miss Effie said,
"Mothers outside."*

— Max Steele, "The Cat and the Coffee Drinkers"

*"We have kids, though," Celeste said. "That helps a little.
Our lives aren't just our own."*

*"Yes," I said, "except I took them to be the cement of our
family, my marriage, and they turn out to be kids and not
building materials."*

— Greg Jackson, "Dynamics in the Storm"

One year I had a student who struggled socially and
emotionally and whose mother, in the middle of the year, was
succumbing to cancer. She was too sick to make it to parent-
teacher conferences, and I knew that, but what I didn't know
was that her husband would show up with a portable
speakerphone to try to include her in their son's presentation
of his work. At first he had trouble establishing a connection,
but finally we heard her weak voice on the line, and all three
of us leaned close to the phone when we talked so she could
hear. My student's father used a pet name for his wife, as if I
wasn't there. I led another parent conference once in which

the father belittled his son on the spot for spending all his time in his room *pretending* to write music, and that was heartbreaking too. I've had parents who made my day—my year—by approaching me with beaming faces and saying, I've wanted to meet you; my daughter won't stop talking about your class. I've had other parents—same year—join battles over specific grades their child received on a specific task. There are parents whose default position toward teachers is generosity. There are parents whose default position is suspicion. There are parents who make you want to bring your A game every day. After a tedious field trip that was hard to organize and harder to manage, they send you a note saying how grateful they are that you put in the work to give their kids a great experience, and that one note braces you to want to do it all over again even though it consumes far too much of your time. When you organize an event to showcase student work, they show up, these parents, and they bring a family friend, and they find you out before they leave to say, I know we've met, but I wanted to reintroduce myself. I'm Molly's mother, and she's having a great year. Thanks for arranging things like this for us to see what our kids are learning. And you vow to do it again with this same group because of that simple gratitude. There are parents who, after a complex event you organize for the students, send a long email that pours water on your triumph, because their kid was up until four in the morning finishing a project, and almost no visitors stopped at their table to hear their presentation. There are parents who send emails that begin with apologies for taking up your time. There are parents who write multi-screen emails outlining the flaws in your whole approach. There are parents who critique your teaching by comparing you to one of your colleagues. There are parents who ask if there's anything they can do to help. There are parents who ask why you're not doing more. Parents are the teacher's biggest ally and the biggest headache. I've known many teachers who admit out loud that they don't like to deal with parents at all. They got into teaching to work with young people.

The range of parent personalities is as wide and various as human nature, but one thing unites them, and it's the thing every teacher has to make herself remember: they love their child more than even great teachers can, and all the energy they bring to their interactions at school are freighted with their hopes and especially their anxieties. Some of the best advice I've received about dealing with parents is to try to figure out what they're really anxious about, even to ask specific questions: "If your child doesn't get an A in this class, what is it you're worried about happening?" I had a parent of a 7th grader once who was worried that anything less than an A would disrupt their plan of sending their son to Exeter, and from there to M.I.T., at which point I asked if their son was also invested in that plan. "Doesn't matter," I was told. "That's what he needs to be prepared for." Sometimes questions like, "Have you ever seen what I'm describing to you at home, or in other classes before?" will open a floodgate of anxiety or emotion. Questions let the parent talk, and usually they just want to be heard. The best advice I have for younger teachers is to remember that parent anger when it comes is often parent fear, and that anxiety for their child's success is usually what brings them to your door.

School counselors and psychologists can tackle the finer points of parent stress, but I offer this as a teacher's best strategy: Get out of in front of any parent anxiety by having positive, celebratory interactions early and often. When I moved to New York, we began the school year in some disarray. Schedules were a mess, culture was uncertain, and protocols and practices were being built on the fly. I was on two teams of teachers: a sixth-grade and a seventh-grade team. Both struggled to settle students down into new routines. In the middle of all that, the sixth-grade team was working hard to engage students with interesting, experiential projects and tasks. In history, we built those caves in classrooms and decorated the inside to look like the ancient caves at Lascaux, while the outside we decorated with graffiti to look like New York City. As part of a unit on the flawed heroes of the ancient world, we took Styrofoam wig heads and made Janus-faced figures, depicting both virtues and failures. In English, students memorized short speeches from Shakespeare's *Julius Caesar.* They were writing their own plays too. And as that work progressed, we decided as a team to host an evening for parents to exhibit the student efforts. We were proud of the kids, and we thought the parents would be too, but also, and importantly for us at the time, we wanted to build a bridge to the parents in that grade. It was a brand-new school. We all had anxieties and uncertainties. You could feel the stress as mid-term approached. The sixth-grade head teacher called the parent rep, put her on speaker phone, and said, if we host this event, do you think people will come? Several of us sat around that iPhone, nervous even to try this event. But the parent rep told us to go for it; she'd do her best to generate interest. So we ordered some refreshments and set up in our common space all the ancient wig heads, complete with explanatory biographies, and we gathered the kids, in simple costumes, for their Shakespeare speeches. As 6:00 approached, no one was there. Not a single parent had come. We looked at each other and shrugged, panicked a little, and kept organizing the kids to get ready for their parts. Then at 6:00 exactly, the elevator doors opened, and two full cars of parents stepped out. Then more came. Then more. The security guard had held them all at the door until that moment. We had a capacity crowd.

Looking back, it seems less important what we did that night than that we just did *something* that night. Students showed off their wig-head work, recited their Shakespeare speeches, sat in small groups to read their plays. When we had everyone together at the end, we told parents what the unit was focused on and what we were trying to learn and what we were going to do next and what the rest of the year was about, and we had some music, student music, and then we mingled and drank fruit water and introduced ourselves to individual parents. It was a night that built community and a night that built relationships. Though I know it's hyperbole, and that as the year went on we had the usual struggles and misunderstandings, and made the usual mistakes as teachers, and had our bad days, I sometimes told people that after that night we could do no wrong. By which I meant, the parents knew and trusted us, and we knew them, and so we built on that connection and shared experience whatever else came up. In fact, late that year—I'm just remembering this as I write—when we were working on a final project to exhibit, one of our best students had a hard time focusing, and he complained to his parents about what we were asking them to do. The parents sent me a long, challenging email. I asked them to come in to talk. Before I cleared up the substance of the misunderstanding and the creative interpretation of their son of what we were doing, I said to the father, David, I have to say I was surprised to get your email because I know you know us, and you know all we've done for your son this year—because his son had some difficulties that required our team to surround him and help him and draw out his best self—I'm just surprised, I told him, that you wouldn't give us the benefit of the doubt and assume we weren't doing anything except trying to give the kids a great experience. The expression on the faces of these two very lovely, very smart, very wonderful, very engaged parents changed. We shifted ground. We talked about the project. We moved on. And I think we had the conversation we had because of that earlier showcase evening. We weren't just solving a problem; we were advancing an existing relationship. That parent and I stayed in regular touch until the son graduated six years after. I still think of them with fondness.

CLARITY AND GRANDEUR

Our one aim is to intensify the powers of thinking and of feeling in those whom we teach; and the only method we have of doing this is to open, through countless ways, every possible avenue to thought, emotion and expression and to keep ourselves alive as we are doing so.

— Mary Ellen Chase, "The Teaching of English"

In an interview available on YouTube, the actor Mark Rylance talks about his craft in terms of the categories of Greek rhetoric. *Clarity* is number one on the ancient list, he says, but it's followed hard by *grandeur*. Rylance is eager to recover the love of grandeur: "I want to encourage [actors] that the beauty of what they're saying and how they're saying it is as important as the meaning of it, the emotional truth, all the different qualities. We hope that our performances have some soul, and by that I mean that there's some relationship between our physical, material lives and our imaginative, spiritual lives, whatever that relationship may be."

If I had to plant a flag on a hilltop and defend it with my last musket shot, it would look something like what Mark Rylance describes here: teaching has to have soul, it has to aspire to be beautiful as well as clear, it should be inspiring and not just measurably effective. Clarity is crucial as a condition of success, but it is not what success looks like. Call it the building in which we reside. But school is the life inside the educational structure, and teachers, like Rylance's actors, should be reminded, even in the face of enormous logistical-organizational expectations, that the beauty of what they do is as important as the meaning. Unless this belief is embedded deeply in the mindset of the teacher and deeply in the culture of the school, clarity will not only win the day every time— clarity of achievement results, clarity of aims and expectations, clear marks of progress or improvement—it will crowd out everything else and treat beauty and grandeur as nice luxuries we simply can't afford.

Grandeur in a school is not just about having big artistic performances, though the more of those the better. Grandeur involves attention to the inspiration of the school experience, the feel of it. There should be some sense of what Durkheim attributed to religious experience: collective effervescence— shared inspiration. It can take many forms. I know of one school that gathered in its courtyard every Monday morning for a collective launch to set the tone for the week, then everyone entered school together and began. My school in North Carolina invited all students into the gym on the first day back and had every student make a lap shaking every teacher's hand. My school in New York ended the year with faculty lined along the main staircase, shaking every student's hand as they left for the summer. I was in a middle school where faculty wrote a song and played it at the opening assembly to welcome students to the new school year. I know schools where the seniors write and deliver formal speeches to the student body as part of their exit experience. I watched a team of teachers once build a lineup of assemblies that always began with student musical performances. These rituals and ceremonies, big and small, remind students that they are part of a noble endeavor, that they are doing more than getting technical training or biding their time for the real stuff of life.

Faculty need this too. Faculty may need this especially. All professional development should build grandeur and beauty into the training, into the work. Faculty should have an abiding sense that they are building skyscrapers and cathedrals, not simply laying bricks. Or to switch the metaphor, teachers who feel their job is like pruning and watering a single tree might lose sight of the sweeping forest around them. We need to remind ourselves over and over what that sweeping purpose is, because if we lose sight of it for ourselves, if we have no vision for the grandeur, we will translate a small sense of purpose to students. Everything we ask students to do should be framed with larger visions and purposes. Telling that story over and over is what makes teaching a bracing and even profound experience, rather than an important but tedious one. We should ask ourselves again and again, what are we really here to do? The answer should sound more like poetry than handbook prose.

The danger of advocating grandeur is the same danger in describing teaching as art: it can sound soft around the edges to people who are reassured of a teacher's effectiveness only in terms of measurable results. Grandeur needs clarity as a second wing for flight, but if we're in danger of overemphasizing one of these virtues anytime soon, it just is not the former.

My favorite projects I've been a part of as a teacher have all cared about attention to grandeur. I was on a sixth-grade humanities team once that studied the ancient world using two framing questions: what is the good life, and what makes a good society? We thought this focus on goodness would keep our study relevant—lifeworthy. We built units around the questions: Were Athens and Sparta both good societies in their way? Or did we want to make some judgments? Which ancient figures or ancient cultures best captured what a good life looks like? In the play *Julius Caesar*, did noble Brutus make a good decision? In what sense was Marc Antony's loyalty good? Those kinds of questions. We wanted to end the year with an exhibition of student work, but we wanted to do something new. We wanted them to transfer their understanding to a new context, a new challenge. So we organized what we called the School of Athens capstone project. We showed students the famous painting by Raphael and did a little background study of the work. Who were all these people depicted? Why Athens? Then we assigned them each to be a figure in the painting. Their task was to answer our essential course question—what is a good life?—from the perspective of the historical figure, then from their own perspective. We asked them to write speeches from those two points of view, one minute each. They would deliver those speeches in front of an audience of parents and faculty in the final week of school.

Then we got ambitious. We decided we wanted to project an image of the painting behind the students and have them create their own version of it in the foreground. We had a space where this seemed possible on a landing below the cafeteria. We spoke with the building supervisors about closing off the open space with the firewalls so it would feel like a small theater. We had students get props to match the figures in the painting (a compass, a book, a globe). They established the pose of their respective figures, organized simple costumes. And then, on the night of the event, with parents assembled in makeshift seats, and faculty standing along the rails above and all around, one by one the students broke out of the tableau and introduced themselves: *I am Aristotle, and to me the good life is....* Having finished the first speech, the student turned to a different pose and continued: *I am Graham, and to me the good life is....* Thirty-six kids made their speeches. Parents were moved to hear their son or daughter express an incipient vision of the world. Teachers were pleased by the shifting perspectives and the confident presentations. It's been almost ten years now, and we sometimes still talk about that night.

And you could ask yourself what purpose the projected painting served and all the effort to recreate it? You could ask whether students couldn't have demonstrated the same amount of learning by standing in a classroom in jeans and sweatshirts—and used their rehearsal time and the attention to the exhibition for learning other things. I had a falling out with a colleague over questions exactly like these. These capstone projects are nice, she told me, but our kids needed to work more on their reading skills. We couldn't afford to do projects like these until their reading levels were higher. There were, after all, only so many instructional hours in the school year. We had to focus our priorities differently. Things like the School of Athens simply took too much time.

Maybe she was right. Teachers have honest disagreements over the best use of limited time. A group of us insisted on valuing the shared experience of something meaningful and grand. We worked hard to get students to take those speeches seriously and to compress their understanding into a presentable form. That did take time. So did the rehearsals for getting kids to hold their poses, to know who they followed, to speak with authority and clarity and life, to practice being still and listening while fellow students spoke. It took time, and it took more energy than a classroom lesson would have. We did it anyway. We were after other things. We might have been wrong. But we had a vision. We wanted students to be swept up in an exhibition that attended to detail and beauty as well as substance. Clarity and grandeur. It felt right to us. It was good enough for the Greeks.

MY TEACHING LIFE

The same old role, the role that is what we make it, as great as we like,
Or as small as we like, or both great and small.

—— Walt Whitman, "Crossing Brooklyn Ferry"

I wasn't living the life I thought I would be living as I turned forty. I thought I would be writing novels, publishing them. And I tried, but in the end I couldn't get the writing to work, and because that's what I had aspired to do, because that's what I saw when I projected a successful life ahead, I couldn't decide whether it was heroic or foolish to keep struggling to write. If my inner world and my sense of myself wobbled, my teaching world by the time I turned forty was steady and consistent. I was in a groove. I felt confident and sturdy. I'd been teaching the same curriculum for about five years, and while every year we tweaked something, and every year I tried to add one new thing, some new historical case study or biography, I could, every August, give you the rough outline of how the year would unfold: major units, projects, experiences, assessments. It was a program that engaged students and that was fun to teach. We were happy with it. School was good for me; no complaints. Yet still around my tenth year of teaching I hit a wall.

I had three small children at the time. When I turned forty, they were eight, six, and three years old. My daughters were terrific young readers who gave very plain names to their dolls (a special doll was named Special; a favorite stuffed rabbit was Bunny). My son was obsessed with Ford F-150 trucks. He was happy sitting down and just flipping through the Ford catalogue. My wife stayed home with the kids and took in a friend's small children for extra income. We lived in a small three-bedroom ranch house in a neighborhood of brick homes built in the 1950s. Every few months I had to crawl through a narrow door commando-style, to get under the house to change the HVAC filter. Beside the duct was the skeleton of a dead mouse I never disturbed. I mowed the big lawn with an old riding mower the previous owner left behind. In the fall, it took two full days to rake leaves, clean gutters. In winter, an ice storm once sent a big tree branch crashing onto the roof, stunning us awake. I won a national prize one year for a technology project my colleagues and I created, and I spent my portion of the money getting the slatted carport wall painted. For vacations, we drove the kids to see their grandparents. My '86 Subaru wagon got me back and forth from work. Noble steed. In the narrow tool shop beside the house, I encountered a snake once and darted away—and never entered that space with confidence again. In warm weather, I sometimes grilled burgers or kebabs on the Weber grill we kept on a small brick patio out back. Through the windows, my daughters might be practicing piano. Their toys spread all over the small living room: the wooden train set, the interlocking foam letters, the Playskool sets, the puzzles and cars. At the end of the day they learned to put things back in their baskets, but during the day it was a North Pole workshop floor again. I had a corner glider near the front door where I did my reading. So much reading, well into my thirties, reading not to disappear or distract myself or unwind or simply enjoy, but reading because I remained convinced of some purpose, and even if I wasn't sure exactly what it was, this calling of mine, I thought if it ever decided to show itself books would position me to know it and receive it. They would sharpen my vision against false gods. Well into my thirties, I read and read and read. And at night, my wife and I read books to the kids, and I made a lap to their various beds to sing the same three songs over and over. My son texted me not long ago (he's a teenager now): what's that song you used to sing us that went "home I want to be"? It was a folk song—they never knew this—that I heard a single time as a high school student at the summer program where I met the first girl I really loved, and I never forgot the song because I never forgot her either, this beautiful song about a sailor longing to get home.

In my early days as a teacher, the hours after my kids went to bed would be devoted to more school work—lesson prep or more likely grading—but by my tenth year, I was efficient at school, and I had the drill down, and I was no longer coaching basketball, which drained four months of the year, and I was good at my job, but I wasn't happy. Not really. Some of that was personal: our marriage was struggling, and I wasn't helping figure it out. Some of it was biographical: I was having a hard time reconciling myself to what I'd become, and to the world I inhabited. To love someone fully and to feel loved back, to send confident, decent children into the world to have their shot, to do some job well and to enjoy it, and to see and read and feel interesting things—that does seem to me enough now for a life. That and a stack of books to reread unrushed. But mostly loving and being loved back. I couldn't see that at the time. I told someone I felt like I was in the middle of a long tunnel that bent, and I couldn't see the light behind me and I couldn't see the light ahead, but it seemed right to keep going. I just wasn't sure where the darkness was taking me. For a long time I struggled to sleep.

The year my wife and I separated, I started reviewing books for the local newspaper. There was something earnest and admirable in how I did it. There was also something desperate. When I reached out about the work at first and the editor hesitated, I persisted, crazily pitching books until he assigned me a biography of a Russian writer I loved. I worked as hard on that piece as I would have if I were writing for *The New Yorker*. It ran as the long lead piece on the facing books pages of the Sunday paper. That Monday when I got to school, someone had taped it to the refrigerator in the faculty lounge and written in Sharpie across the top of the page, "Way to go, Shy." That moved me deeply. I started asking for more books to review. Assignments came. I pitched other places and wrote for them too. I threw myself into reviewing books as a second job. My teaching at the time allowed it. I'd been at the school long enough. I had a great schedule that left me a block of afternoon time in which I did all my grading, all my tweaking of lessons, all my photocopying and posting of assignments on our web page, all my emails to parents or colleagues. I taught hard, went to lunch, ate at my assigned table with regular rotations of students, then put my head down and got my work done before a last class at the end of the day. Most of the time, I could do it. With a lot of concentration, I could stay ahead of my work. Then, as soon as school let out, and I waited the half hour we were supposed to wait, or attended afterschool meetings, I'd drive away from school and make it to my coffee shop near the N.C. State campus by 4:00. There, I'd glance at one of the newspapers that were always in the recycling bin by the water cooler. I'd get my coffee and maybe a bagel if I was hungry. I'd finish the bagel, fold away the newspaper, take a deep breath, and pull out the review copy of whatever I'd been assigned and get to work. If I had three weeks to work, I'd spend at least one week reading whatever else I could gather by the author, or any books I knew were like this new one. If I had four weeks, I'd spend two doing this background reading. Because I knew that's what the best reviewers did. They connected the new work to everything that had come before, and they connected it out to other writers today. I was ordering used books all the time, reading everything I could possibly manage. It was like graduate school, but my focus kept shifting every few weeks—self-paced graduate school for someone who couldn't make up his mind.

I always left myself a week to read and reread the assigned book itself; I left at least a full week to write, revise, and submit. Once I got into a pattern and was confident I knew what I was doing, I started lining up multiple assignments at a time. My Raleigh editor would call me on the phone, and we'd talk through a few months of work. I always had something going. My coffee shop, Cup a Joe, was a grungy former auto parts store with cement floors and mismatched tables, a church pew along one wall, a row of connected school desks along another. Local artists hung their work on the brick walls. The owners had a thing for Elvis, and there was Elvis paraphernalia all over. They roasted their own beans. By the front door, when the big roaster was on, and the hot beans spilled down to the grate to spin and cool, you smelled the burn of fresh coffee instead of the second-hand smoke that for years hung like pea soup hipster smog in the adjacent smoking room.

I liked to sit near the front windows. I recognized other regulars, and they recognized me. We made polite eye contact and nodded greetings sometimes, but we didn't talk, or almost never. I put my head down and worked after school until 6:00 or 6:30 every day. If I was in flow, I'd push on past 7:00. Then, if it wasn't the night for me to take my kids out to dinner, I'd go home, eat something simple, watch the news if I hadn't missed it, and settle in to read books for the next review until 9:30 or 10:00. Then an Ambien, then something on TV while the medicine settled, then bed. The alarm woke me at 5:45 so I could get in another hour of work before school the next morning.

I saw my kids every other weekend and once a week for dinner. Other than those visits, these book-review rituals plus teaching were my life. These two jobs had nothing and had everything to do with each other for about five years.

I see myself in the morning walking down the hill from the faculty parking row to the side door of our middle school. I get upstairs before the first students arrive at 7:30. I look over my calendar for the day, make sure I remember meetings and deadlines. Any papers the students need, I had readied and stacked the day before. Alone in my room, maybe I'm already thinking about what I need to do that afternoon in order for tomorrow to be just like this. If I'm showing slides, I'll get the projector on and queued. Before students arrive, I'll get a cup of coffee in the faculty lounge downstairs. When they start pouring into morning room, they will be here for twenty minutes. I have one of the larger rooms, so it's a designated holding pen for half the grade. Usually I put some music on, usually it's jazz, as they enter. I might be responding to early emails. I might be grading another stack of papers if I have a backlog. I might wander around the room just welcoming the kids and making small talk. Maybe somebody had a game the night before. Maybe some of them are in rehearsal for "Peter Pan." Maybe I know they have a science test and tease them for not studying now, or I look over the shoulder of a kid doing math and ask why there are so many letters when math is supposed to use numbers. Maybe I do something whimsical to wake us all up. Maybe I wad up a piece of paper and make a silly pledge to give everyone a homeroom A if I can make this shot from across the room into that corner trash can. Maybe someone is quietly reading, and I ask about the book. Maybe I overhear that it's someone's birthday. Maybe the kids want to sing "Happy Birthday." Even when the rest of my life felt stressful, I still loved being in school for these moments and exchanges. I was thinking about the kids and the community, but I was getting something out of these interactions too. Something human, something personal, at a time when I needed exactly that. And who knows whether my own uncertainties at the time didn't make me more sensitive to these passing human connections. I knew with students around I had nothing to prove, just something to do. I was free with them, in a way, partly because I was unfree on my own, away from them.

I think back to some peers, some of the smartest teachers I ever knew. What versions did they have of hitting a wall? What did they do?

Steven hit it hard. He left a wife and two kids around the same time I did. He felt guilty. He told his wife she could have his entire check, she could have everything. He took a second job at our school as a night guard, driving around the campus in a golf cart. I sat in his class once when he centered a lesson around war-time music. This was during his tough stretch. He launched the lesson with a story: he was a philosophy major in college, and his grandmother was worried about his cynicism. "You listen to happy music," she told him. It moved him to remember it; it moved me to watch him relate it.

As my friend Anthony approached forty, he was feeling stale. He loved the school, he loved and enjoyed his students, but the job was grinding, and too many meetings were tedious. He was an English teacher, and a fresh pile of papers to grade rose from the ashes of every stack completed. He took on some extra duties involving technology integration. He networked in the broader educational community. Maybe something school-related but not classroom teaching would be the right next thing to recharge him and his career. Finally, he made a bold move and just left teaching. He was working on an educational web site, but it was in its early stages and couldn't offer a reliable income. Still, he quit because he needed to do something else. He was spent. One of the happiest members of a school community I've ever known, he just had to move on.

Carole recharged herself by taking on new teaching loads every so often. She entered education after an early career as a consultant. She pioneered the integrated humanities program in our middle school, then crossed the quad to join the upper

school and build more programs there. A first-rate English
teacher, she started a debate team that became one of the
school's shining stars. For a while she taught seniors, then she
came back to eleventh grade to do A.P. classes for juniors. A
relentless intellectual and a formidable personality, she didn't
suffer fools, but also, at the same time, she gave you all her
heart. I talked with her a lot over the years, and she would
pivot instantly if she realized I was in difficulty. She'd stop
joshing and joking and ask quiet questions until I got out
what I needed to say. She didn't pander, though. She told me
exactly what she thought. That's how she did with students,
too, on their papers. It was blunt but never cold. Her
certainty made up for my insecurities and hesitations. For a
while, when the weather found the sweet spot of mid-late
spring, she and I would meet on the school track every so
often to walk and get exercise and talk about whatever came
up. The fertility of her mind made her one of the best
teachers I've ever known, also a terrific friend. But she kept
herself on the move a little too, to stay fresh, to keep that rich
mind in motion. She didn't like it if an administrator got in
the way of her imaginative shifts and experiments. One of the
times she listened to me was when I was on the fence about
taking the job in New York City. You should definitely go,
she told me right off. Her opinion was instant and
unequivocal. Except that then she heard something lost in my
voice, I think, which made her shift gears to find out what
was really going on. I did go to New York, in the end, and we
stayed in touch. She was the one I called that night I couldn't
figure out what to do with a very messy group of 7th graders. I
called her whenever I was unsure of myself. It devastated me
when she got leukemia. The last time we spoke she was giving
me relationship advice. I said, Carole, we don't need to be
talking about this; you're not well. She brushed that off. This
is the best thing I could do right now, she said. Let me help
you one more time. What's going on? I *still* imagine her voice
and her life when I'm stuck. What would Carole say? And
why isn't she still here to help me one more time?

Lydia was Carole's equal as an intellect and teacher. In fact, she took over Carole's job when Carole moved on to the high school. Lydia did that eventually too, then she moved to L.A. to take a teaching job there before getting restless and going back to school to study advertising. A brilliant writer with impeccable wit, I think Lydia felt constrained by the teaching world. She worked for big advertising firms, but last time we communicated she had gone out on her own, freelancing. To my delight, she was trying to write.

The motions of creative, vibrant minds. How to hold those in classrooms in a way that lets them flourish? Carole kept moving around. Lydia kept moving on. Anthony exercised patience in one spot, but finally left. Steven broke. I added to my stable school world a ridiculously paced second world, reviewing books. But one colleague remained.

Did my friend Dave, who I celebrated earlier, ever hit a wall? Not that anyone would know. His projects, though, are so elaborate and so detailed—the packet for his Senate simulation, in which students conduct multiple legislative sessions and have their own cloak room and follow procedures to a tee, is a small-town phone book—and the energy he pours into running the student news broadcast or coaching sports or taking students on optional road trips to historical sites over school breaks, all of it expresses a level of creativity that could easily have found other channels. A talented man with a ranging mind, he also left college thinking he'd write a novel. He tried too, just like I did. Neither of us pulled it off. Then his life started moving in other directions: marriage, a move east from San Francisco, a job at a brand-new school with blank-slate possibilities, eventually two children. He didn't follow Carole to the high school. He didn't follow Anthony or Lydia to other fields of work. He didn't follow me to New York City. He never, ever looked like someone tired of the job. And I fantasize returning for his retirement party. I want to say how highly I think of him, how much it meant to have someone like that at the other end of the hall, inciting life in students every year, how much it still means to me to think of him there. What a steady gift teachers like Dave are to students and to schools.

I'm thinking of all these colleagues as I think about the arc of my teaching career. It's helpful to see how these brilliant people measured out their life differently. It means there's no one model for how to do this job well and how to flourish in it. I still don't understand all my own peculiar choices. Mid-career, I hit a wall. It didn't keep me from loving kids, teaching well. It may have made those better.

I reviewed books hard for five years, then I stopped. I wanted to try a longer writing project again. Then my ex-wife remarried, and she and my children moved, and we had a hard year. I wasn't sure whether to leave North Carolina or stay, to go back to reviewing books or try something else. That summer, I was sitting in my coffee shop near N.C. State reading the Sunday *New York Times*, when I saw an article about a new school opening in New York City. I tucked it away to ponder and research later. Something in me rose to the idea of that school, the challenge, the fresh start, New York City. I was exhausted, personally and professionally. But I was ready to try again, I thought. Thoreau at the end of *Walden*: "I left the woods for as good a reason as I went there. Perhaps it seemed to me that I had several more lives to live, and could not spare any more time for that one." I moved to New York City.

The details of our life are hidden from our students and for the most part hidden from our fellow teachers. But we bring all of ourselves to the work. We don't compartmentalize; we sublimate. Still, all of it is there in every lesson, in every exchange with a student, in every conversation with a colleague between classes. We teach with our whole life—not as material to bring into the classroom, but as a sense of the world, a feeling about it, an attitude toward it, a way of seeing and being that is, if we're lucky, contagious with wisdom and joy and love.

After twenty-one years in the classroom, I made a move to a leadership position in our school. I wanted to see if all the virtues of great teaching could translate to good leadership. Everything I've described here as the heart of great teaching should ripple out as the portrait of a great school—I think. With everything in me, I try to tend to that vision of what school is for. Friends, it is much harder than it looks.

I plan to keep teaching too. I want to be a school leader who helps teachers become their best selves and who helps build a community around the right things, but I also hope to go on keeping a foot in the classroom. I didn't go into teaching way back because I had an excited vision for transforming students. I hesitated, I looked around, it seemed my best option, and I tried. I got better and more confident—as I got more competent—and then I began to understand what was really worth doing in the work, saw the beauty of watching an indifferent student turn on to something—anything—or a student who likes to play it safe for a grade who takes a risk on something—anything—or the smile on the face of a student when I praise some unexpected effort or insight or choice, the sheepish "thank you," the repressed delight, maybe even the birth of a sense of herself. The thrill of teaching is seeing kids wake up, in their thousand different ways, and it won't be every kid with you, but it will be some, and it's moving and so powerful that Tolstoy could only describe it this way: we have no right to see it. It's that remarkable, and personal.

Yet we get to.

TEACHING LIFE

*The simplest words—we do not know what they mean
except when we love and aspire.*

—— Emerson

Dear Emily and Katie,

I began this work thinking about you both as potential young teachers. I've wandered all over the place trying to say everything I know—your father's disorganized inheritance. It's for you, and it's for anybody in your shoes, wondering what kind of job this really is. It's for teachers no matter their years on the job. It's for parents who have kids in schools, or anybody who cares about making school a rich experience. Books about school and school performance are often studies in anxiety. Books about teaching should be hopeful corrections.

I haven't covered everything here. I haven't tried to anticipate all the specific challenges you'll face: discipline issues (alas), budget crunches, unhelpful colleagues, aloof or micro-managing administrators, unreasonable parents, disrespectful kids, great work going unnoticed by anyone eligible to vote, mounds of grading, homework of your own, kids coming to school sick and getting you sick, summers off to find part-time jobs, standards and assessments that make school seem like a space shuttle launch. It's a tough job. I know that. I've worked in mostly privileged schools, and still I've hit walls more than once. But I decided not to focus on tactics and strategies here. What I wanted to offer was a portrait of what teaching is really for. Because if you get that established up front, if you're steering toward the right star, you can figure out how to handle the obstacles and the weather you encounter every day. You'll go on waking students up to themselves and to an interesting world and then mobilizing their interest and their life. You'll laugh a lot, and you'll challenge them hard, and you'll try to figure out who they are so you can help them figure out who they can become. You'll recommend books. You'll praise and encourage when they need it, and you'll rebuke and admonish when they need that instead. All the time you'll be thinking about the full biography inside every kid in front of you. You'll make all of it personal, but you'll take none of it personally. And you can always call me when you have a bad day. I have some experience there too. Anyway, other people far less remarkable than you have done this work. You'll be more than fine. You'll flourish.

And now if you'll indulge me as I close, I want to pay tribute to the profession itself. From the outside, people do recognize the value of what we do, but it doesn't always feel ennobling. Teachers are like firefighters and police officers and nurses: how grateful we are that people do these jobs; how little we envy them. It's other teachers who will shore up your morale and your belief in the work. The best teaching years I've had have always been a product of having great colleagues. In great schools, teachers feel like teams. All of you see yourselves as teaching all of the kids. It's collective, community effort, and you delight in each other's talents and successes and shore up each other's weaknesses. That communal aspect of great schools is what makes the job nourishing as well as meaningful. You can give and give to your students in any context, and that can be heroic, but you need to get something back to stay healthy and full, and for that you need your colleagues, not your students. I'll even say that while we should aim for student-centered classrooms, we should build teacher-centered schools, for that reason. My best colleagues used to remind me that it's good for the students to see that teachers like working together. My best colleagues popped in and out of each other's classrooms, encouraging the shared work as it was happening, not just behind the scenes. The health of the faculty is the condition for the growth of the students. It's like the airplane instruction to put the oxygen mask on yourself first before tending to infants and children. Teacher-centered schools give lots of oxygen to their faculties, and those teachers, buoyed themselves, set students up for transformative experiences. That's school. So, be a good colleague. Build other people up. Put yourself on teams to do interesting things.

Watching your colleagues will be a big part of your own development as a teacher. I haven't mentioned an important book yet, but maybe it's good that I saved it for the end: *The World Beyond Your Head: On Becoming an Individual in an Age of Distraction* by Matthew B. Crawford. Crawford's attention to "embodied perception" is a good balancing weight to my enthusiastic and, if I'm not careful, weightless Emersonianism! Crawford argues that the way we find ourselves and flourish in the world is through submission to living practices in real communities. The discipline and attention of apprenticeship builds competence, which builds real freedom and joy. In that spirit, as you give yourselves over to learning this craft of teaching, watch the master teachers. Don't close your door when things are hard; go find the veterans. Commiserate. Debrief. Kick around ideas. Ask questions. Your deepest joy over the years will be your quirky, vulnerable, inspiring, unpredictable students. But right behind your students is the joy of being part of a community sharing a craft. Lean on your colleagues. Watch what they do. Steal their best tricks.

I want to go on writing things as a way to keep you company myself, but it's time to let you go and figure your own way ahead. I guess that sets up a final quick lesson: end well. Whatever you're doing, end things well; finish strong: a single lesson, a school year, a job, a stint in a city, a friendship. End things well. It gives you momentum for the next thing. And we're always, all of us, all the time, moving on, turning pages, advancing down an open road. We keep moving forward with new students, new years, new colleagues, sometimes new schools. You can't teach and not pay attention to the way that everything goes on wheeling ahead—without our consent. It makes me melancholy. But it also makes me sure that if we're not trying to teach *life*, the whole moving experience of it, we're missing the point of the work. I know that won't be either of you.

And how could we be here already, you as adults ready to teach other people's children, and not children yourselves, coming home on the last day of kindergarten, telling me in our little house about "the work," or that PTA event where the visiting artist played an instrument that seemed to have a hundred parts like something Dick Van Dyke would play, and we all sang along, or going to Golden Corral on Tuesday nights because two of us could eat for 99 cents if the other two were full price, and on my teacher's salary that price was right, and we always sat in Bob's section there because he remembered us and had a kind of zany warmness about him that we liked and looked forward to and later missed, or the way you helped up the player from the other team at a soccer game, Emily, when that team was just destroying you all— you helped her up as if kindness were just matter-of-fact to you, and it's still unforgettable to me—or the last day of seventh grade, Katie, you as a student, me as a teacher, when we hugged and recognized the privilege of having been inside each other's school worlds that way for the year, and who gets to do that? We got to do that. And me wanting now to go back there to repeat all of it over and over and hold us all there and appreciate it more and love it more and do it all better, but how could anything possibly improve on what you became? It couldn't. So, keep going.

And don't forget to take a picture of yourself on the first day of every new school year. Make an album for your own sake and your old dad's. If I could sit in the back of your classrooms and cheer you on across the years, I would. But you won't need me. Anyway, that's sort of what I've been doing in these pages all along.

RECOMMENDED READING

In my ideal school, teachers would pause for half an hour every school day, stop whatever they were doing, and just read something because they wanted to. It might relate to education; it might not. It might relate to something they were teaching; it wouldn't have to. They would take their book with a mug of coffee into a quiet space where students could observe them reading for pleasure, for nourishment, for life. If an administrator walked by, teachers wouldn't tuck the book away and pretend to be doing something more important. They would keep reading because it was made clear to them long before that reading was as important as anything they could be doing. If half an hour passed and a teacher was so absorbed in her book she kept on, the administrator would smile and keep walking. In my ideal school.

Here is a partial list-in-progress of some books that have helped inspire my own thinking about teaching. I offer it as a conversation starter rather than a canon. They are books that relate to my own project here to think about mindset and our relationship to our work. There is much, much more to be said. May the list multiply in a dozen directions.

Bob Blaisdell, Editor
Essays on Teaching

This treasure trove of essays runs the gamut from Plato to Billy Collins and includes the Emerson and Tolstoy I reference so often in this book. The beginning of any good library on teaching.

William James
Talks to Teachers on Psychology: And to Students on Some of Life's Ideals

If James were giving you directions to his house, I think the instructions would tremble with generosity and grace. These talks to teachers ennoble the profession by taking it seriously and philosophically; they nourish teachers by caring about their success. I held up two of my seminary professors as models of the great poles of teaching: inspiration and recognition—waking students up and also "getting" them, making them feel known. James is both those modes in a single voice, a single mind. If you read James and don't think teaching is a high calling, you should probably go back to square one.

James Baldwin
"A Talk to Teachers"

Baldwin's talk, sandwiched in time between the March on Washington and the Kennedy assassination, feels as urgent today as it was in 1963. Baldwin demands honest scrutiny of the past and sees education as a vehicle for correcting false, unjust narratives and for inciting reform. The foundation of education, in Baldwin's view, involves cultivating autonomous young people, "to create in a person the ability to look at the world for himself, to make his own decisions.... To ask questions of the universe, and then learn to live with those questions." But having developed that sense of self, Baldwin insists that students go on to "examine society and try to change it and to fight it—at no matter what risk," because this "is the only way societies change."

Ralph Waldo Emerson
"Education"

Like a lot of students, I found Emerson too flowery, too sugary, too *something* when I read him in high school. Let's stop assigning him there. Let's tell students there's this essayist they should remember to get to in their twenties or thirties, when their early ideals have been qualified by experience and disappointment but they're not yet ready to be jaded or cynical. Then read Emerson. Tell them to start with "The Poet" and "Experience" and "Circles"—or whatever it is for you. Tell them they need a ranging canon of their own but to include Emerson somewhere on their shelf as a spur to have a vision of the world, as a reminder to affirm something. And send all young teachers to the compilation of talks grouped together as "Education," where Emerson charges us to inspire, inflame, and awaken students to their life. "The imagination must be addressed," he declares, reminding us, meanwhile, that we need large imaginations ourselves to do this work.

Leo Tolstoy
"Who Is to Teach Whom to Write, We the Peasant-Children or the Peasant-Children Us?"

In *Anna Karenina,* Tolstoy's alter ego Levin is in a conversation with his neighbor about social problems and reforms. The neighbor sees educating the peasants as key. "But how will schools help?" Levin asks. The neighbor responds: "They'll give them different needs." Tolstoy ran schools for the children of local peasants on his estate, and he wrote about the experience in the essay "Who Is to Teach Whom to Write?" In his famous novel, Tolstoy describes Anna Karenina herself as being "filled with the joy of life." That describes Tolstoy the teacher too. He is charmed, he is delighted, he is moved by his young students. And he doesn't stress about what the kids don't know; he nourishes and relishes signs of imagination. This isn't everything we need as teachers, but it's the beginning of everything we need.

Alison Gopnik
The Gardener and the Carpenter: What the New Science of Child Development Tells Us about the Relationship between Parents and Children

Gopnik is a psychologist, and this book targets parents more than teachers, but her main idea is as relevant for classrooms as the home: We adults should not be carpenters crafting children into a version of something we believe in; we should see ourselves as gardeners creating conditions in which children can grow and flourish. Gopnik's progressive vision is a rebuttal of helicopter parenting and tiger-mom child rearing, and I agree with every word she wrote, even as I wonder how this kind of progressive openness translates across the socio-economic spectrum. I wonder the same thing about my own educational vision.

Adrienne Rich
"Claiming an Education"

In this convocation address delivered at Douglass College in 1977, Rich combines a critique of the "almost total erasure of women's experience and thought from the curriculum" with a call for students to embrace "the experience of taking responsibility toward yourselves." For teachers, whether we're at the college level or not, the opening paragraph belongs on our quote boards and door posts: "If university education means anything beyond the processing of human beings into expected roles, through credit hours, tests, and grades (and I believe that in a women's college especially it might mean much more), it implies an ethical and intellectual contract between teacher and student. This contract must remain intuitive, dynamic, unwritten; but we must turn to it again and again if learning is to be reclaimed from the depersonalizing and cheapening pressures of the present-day academic scene."

Mark Edmundson
Teacher: The One Who Made the Difference

This memoir is my favorite portrait of an individual teacher. Edmundson, an English professor at the University of Virginia, describes his high school philosophy instructor Frank Lears as "dealing cards from another deck" and as the teacher who woke him up to see himself in a bold new way—and to see the possibilities of the world differently. Lears had this effect on Edmundson gradually and patiently: a snowball fight here, a book recommendation there, a recognition of the importance of music to his young students and his suggestions that they do something with that interest. "Teachers who matter," Edmundson writes, "sow seeds like this all the time." I love that description: *teachers who matter*. The takeaway from this beautifully written memoir: be one of those.

Mark Edmundson
Why Teach?: In Defense of a Real Education

Edmundson's meditations address a college context explicitly, but the concerns trickle down to every grade below. Education is not preprofessional preparation, he insists, but soul-making: "what we want is real learning—learning that will help us see the world anew and show us that there could be more to our lives than we had thought." Everyone in the profession should read the section of the book headed *Fellow Teachers*. Uncool teachers, he writes there, to take one example of many, get students to see the world in different ways: "The philosophy prof steps in through the window the first day of class and asks her students to write down the definition of the word *door.*"

Michelle Kuo
Reading with Patrick: A Teacher, a Student, and a Life-Changing Friendship

A Harvard grad joins Teach for America and goes to the Arkansas Delta to work with small-town students. When one of her former students, Patrick, kills someone, she returns from law school to find out what happened and to reconnect with him. While the book casts one more spotlight on issues of injustice in America, and is a vivid portrait of stasis and struggle in the rural South, for teachers this memoir offers a moving account of one of their own not giving up on a student in need. Kuo moves back to Arkansas and tutors her now-convicted former student, and in the process he discovers his voice and himself the old-fashioned way—through reading and writing. Kuo comments on a poem of Patrick's: "No trick, no magic, no God could reverse the past, undo what happened: un-kill a man, bring life back, or give Patrick the chance to live his teenage years again. But poetry, or this poem, had brought him closer to a feeling, a presence, to an immensity that could swallow death and do away with time. As supernatural as it all felt, it was just the memory of love: his mother waiting for him to come home."

Ta-Nehisi Coates
Between the World and Me

In this heralded memoir, Coates describes his voracious reading years at Howard University and the professors who deepened his perspectives. He dove into his studies, he tells us, "imagining history to be a unified narrative, free of debate, which, once uncovered, would simply verify everything I had always suspected." His history professors had other ideas, challenging Coates to see complexity and contradiction where he sought coherence, disabusing him, he writes "of my weaponized history." Though this book is about much, much more than school, the role of a teacher meeting a student where he is and then moving him somewhere else is powerfully and wonderfully drawn.

Neil Postman
The End of Education: Redefining the Value of School

If our answer to the question about why kids need to go to school is too small, we will lose their attention and lose our best teachers. Our current answers, Postman says, are too small. We've replaced any meaningful narrative about the purpose of school with "the engineering of learning." We're preparing students for a marketplace, preparing them to use new tools and technologies but not inspiring them with a vision of how to go on shaping themselves, the world, and their own culture. I don't love jeremiads. Or maybe, I think we have too many of them. We need to sing in a range of keys. After the diagnosis and complaint, Postman does change registers, offering big compelling themes for schools to organize learning around—"Spaceship Earth," "The Fallen Angel," "The American Experiment"—which, to this teacher anyway, seem rich with possibility.

Kwame Anthony Appiah
The Ethics of Identity

Identity, diversity, race, pluralism, all these are as urgent in schools as they are in the larger country. The quest for collective projects and collective justice and what Appiah comfortably calls "soul making" inside those larger commitments is an ongoing conversation. We're all joined in it. Appiah eschews easy answers and offers rich, ranging, learned philosophical foundations for that dialogue.

James M. Banner, Jr., and Harold C. Cannon
The Elements of Teaching

This short book gets everything right about teaching, focusing our attention on the teacher herself and what she must be, insisting at every turn that the great teacher provokes students to "surpass themselves," to achieve something like an expanded, beautiful life. The authors stake their claims on these nine attributes of great teachers: learning, authority, ethics, order, imagination, compassion, patience, character, and pleasure. And while the composite portraits they offer of teachers who illustrate these traits feel a little too much like composites, I'd slip this book into the orientation bag of every new teacher I know.

Parker J. Palmer
The Courage to Teach: Exploring the Inner Landscape of a Teacher's Life
This one may belong in a category all its own. Palmer's exploration of the inner life of the teacher makes my own meditations here possible at all and reminds us that the work to make great schools begins always with teachers themselves. Palmer's soul-searching ambition expands the popular idea of teaching the whole child: "I no longer teach to [my students'] imputed ignorance, having rejected that assessment as both inaccurate and self-serving. Instead, I try to teach to their fearful hearts, and when I am able to do so, their minds often come along as well."

John McPhee
The Headmaster
This old-school portrait of an old-school leader, Frank Boyden of Deerfield Academy, offers glimpses of a certain New England boarding school world that is alternately quaint, compulsive, eccentric, and inspired. Boyden leaving a meeting to take a five-minute nap, or riding his horse and buggy in town (and his golf cart around the Deerfield campus), or playing on his school's sports teams—as headmaster—or stooping over to pick up stray paper are all winning, even as Boyden retreats, to this reader, as a man very much (and understandably) of his time, not ours. But the heart of his effectiveness feels timeless. "I believe in boys," he says, when asked for his philosophy. McPhee elaborates: "He seemed to know when there was something in a boy when on the surface there appeared to be nothing." We should still build schools around *that*.

Dana Goldstein
The Teacher Wars: A History of America's Most Embattled Profession

Race, gender, politics, class, money; common schools, testing, charters, Teach for America: all of it is covered in this historical overview. I haven't tried to take on systems and structures in my reflections here. For one thing, I don't feel remotely qualified. Also, it would make for a different book. I want teachers to be inspired by the possibilities of the craft, to make a worthy teaching life inside whatever classroom or structure they're part of. But understanding how our own small story fits inside the frame of the larger story around us and the longer story behind us is one of the merits of this accessible historical survey.

Ken Bain
What the Best College Teachers Do

This study of college professors is fascinating for the way it even explores the question of great teaching. Bain isn't interested in small measures. He wants to know if teachers inspire students to want to keep learning about their subject. He wants to know whether a teacher is content to lead those who want to be led, or works to bring everyone along. He looks for development of deep learning and metacognitive habits. He wants to know if teachers are being effective at the right thing, or just the things they prefer to teach. I wouldn't want this book in the absence of thick descriptions like Mark Edmundson's portrait of his most influential teacher. Start there. But I'd put it on the same shelf for later.

Robert D. Richardson
Splendor of Heart: Walter Jackson Bate and the Teaching of Literature

This portrait of a college professor by an award-winning biographer is full of gusto and warmth. Richardson's teacher—his personality as well as his thinking—seeped into his mind the way Diogenes long ago seeped into mine. Walter Jackson Bate lived for literature and saw in its expression a better mirror of life. Like William James (the subject of one of Richardson's biographies), Bate is large-hearted and generous, inspiring his students and his readers toward their own best lives and selves: "No one puts down Bate's *Johnson* feeling beaten, discouraged, overmatched, or outshone. One finishes the book and, putting it down gently, thinks, 'Very well. Now let us see what *I* can do.'" Whitman hooking his arm around your shoulder, pointing to your own Open Road.

Jane Tompkins
A Life in School: What the Teacher Learned

This memoir by a Duke University professor examines approaches to teaching at all ages. Her portraits of her own early school life are wonderful, but her mature reflections as a professor are even more charged with wisdom: "My point is that classroom learning can constrict a person's horizons even as it broadens them. Learning too well the lessons of the classroom exacts a price. Its exclusive emphasis on the purely intellectual and informational aspects of learning, on learning as individualistic and competitive, can create a lopsided person: a person who can process information efficiently, summarize accurately, articulate ideas, and make telling points; a person who is hardworking, knows how to please those in authority, and who values high performance on the job above all things." Then she goes for the kill: "Everything I have learned in the last ten years has shown me that this is not the sort of person to become. But the educational deck is stacked against becoming anything different."

Frank McCourt
Teacher Man

The writing and voice that made McCourt's memoir *Angela's Ashes* a runaway bestseller are equally vivid here in his account of teaching. McCourt spent three decades in various New York City schools, and his stories of classroom life are bracing. Read this memoir if you've ever anxiously felt students had the real power in the room. Read this if you've ever had to make a quick judgment call—and made the wrong one. Read this if you've been glad to be a teacher but never felt quite like a missionary for the work. Read this if you've doubted yourself—and then surprised yourself on the job. I keep saying books about teaching should be written with more zest and life. McCourt's book tells me to calm down. They're there. Here's one.

Amy Whitaker
Art Thinking: How to Carve out Creative Space in a World of Schedules, Budgets, and Bosses

Whitaker's book is about thinking like an artist in the business world, but her exploration of how to nourish and sustain creativity is more than relevant for educators. Occasionally, she even looks away from the boardroom to the classroom, likening bad teaching to paint-by-number kits: "If you follow these instructions, you will succeed. If you keep your open-ended self in a box, you will rise up the ranks." Her book helps correct the course.

John Stuart Mill
The Autobiography of John Stuart Mill

Mill's father famously turned his young son into a kind of educational experiment, teaching him Greek at the age of three, Latin at the age of eight, isolating him from peers, and cultivating a mindset so rational and intellectual it led to an early breakdown. Mill's self-report is heartbreaking: as he set out to embark on the world, he writes, he was "a well-equipped ship with a rudder, but no sail." James Mill could have benefited from a Victorian version of Alison Gopnik. I use that image of Mill's often when I talk with colleagues about school. It is tempting to focus all our efforts on shipbuilding. The concrete task is always attractive. We want to know exactly what to do, what curriculum to teach, what assessments to give, what measures will assure us we've been successful. But James Mill was successful at rearing a son to stick his marks. John Stuart was a prodigy, a Victorian phenom. But he was also empty and shut down. Schools need wind, and they need sails to catch the wind, and the wind looks like inspiration, like incitement, like curiosity, like beauty, like laughter, like life.

Marilynne Robinson
When I Was a Child I Read Books

No writer I know sounds so different in her essays and her fiction. The novels are gorgeous, patient, hard meditations; the essays polemical elegies: Emily Dickinson meets a very well-read Carrie Nation. I love Marilynne Robinson for taking the world so seriously and for attending to history as the only path to understanding anything at all. More novelists should follow her lead. For teachers, her title essay "When I Was a Child I Read Books," is a wistful and forceful defense of loneliness, and testimony to the way that if we create conditions inside of which young people can flourish and explore, they will learn to be unafraid.

Zadie Smith
"Their Eyes Were Watching God: What Does *Soulful* Mean?"

It was her mother, not a teacher, who pressed the young Zadie Smith to read Zora Neale Hurston, but this coming-of-age essay about Smith's relationship to books and to the dueling pressures of white and black literary traditions, is a reminder that education in the end really is soul work. Since Smith cites her encounter with *Their Eyes Were Watching God*, and Mark Edmundson's pivotal moment with a teacher was a book recommendation, and James Baldwin described his elementary school teacher giving him books to explore, we should remember, as teachers, to stay in the regular simple business of pointing students toward interesting things to read.

Muriel Spark
The Prime of Miss Jean Brodie

Is Miss Brodie the most famous teacher in English-speaking literature? Is it irresponsible to recommend the book to young teachers when the leading lady, still much in her prime, is so flawed and even dangerous, not a little self-important, she who makes a cult of her own set and her own eccentric status? Read it anyway for the prose, the power of the portraits, and the paradox—for teachers, not literary critics—of a big personality who provoked girls toward great things without really setting them free, and who remained unforgettable to anyone she taught.

Colson Whitehead
The Intuitionist

This novel is about elevator inspectors, not teachers, but I can't resist including it here. The book involves a battle of wits between Empiricists and Intuitionists, the empiricists monitoring and evaluating elevator safety via handbooks and protocols, the intuitionists trusting their feel, their judgment. Since an art-science dichotomy goes on at least influencing the teaching landscape, a novel is a good place to see the same dynamic slant.

Richard Rorty
"The Inspirational Value of Great Works"

I quoted from this essay earlier, but I think it deserves an explicit recommendation here. Rorty defends the realm of imagination and inspiration in academia with brio and depth. It's reassuring to know that a struggle to get the vision right for teaching mirrors larger, difficult struggles to get the vision right for thinking at all: about knowledge, about democracy, and about being a human being.

Max Steele
"The Cat and the Coffee Drinkers"

This charming short story set in the Depression-era South involves a small-town teacher named Miss Effie, who runs a famous kindergarten out of her home. People flock to her school because her students always come out reading at a very high level, but before she starts into that core work, she teaches her five and six-year-old charges how to sweep rooms, how to drink coffee, how to shake a hand and give your name—then a false name because sometimes you need to do that with strangers—also, at story's end, how to kill an injured cat. I taught the story for years to my seventh-grade students in North Carolina. The kids found it strange, but they loved it too. One time, the author visited our school, and he began his discussion of the story by asking how many students had ever had a pet. Hands went up. Then he asked how many had had a pet who died. Hands up. Then he asked how many had ever had a grandparent or someone else close in their family die. Slow hands up. I saw in that instant what the story was really for.

Charles Baxter
"Gryphon"

Another short story about a teacher, this one a substitute named Miss Ferenczi, who offers exotic stories to her fourth-grade class, confirms "substitute facts" about mathematical solutions and other phenomena, and, finally, tells student fortunes with a Tarot deck. But this isn't a story about a teacher so much as about how young people experience adults. Here, wonder and curiosity are lit in the narrator, who argues with classmates about what is and isn't true in Miss Ferenczi's ramblings, and tries to convey something of what happened at school to his mother—to no avail. In the end, Miss Ferenczi goes off the rails and is fired. The story asks us to decide whether she achieved something as magical in her three days with these students as the mythical gryphons she describes to them.

The Academy for Teachers
(academyforteachers.org), "Great Writers on Great Teachers"

Sam Swope and his team at the Academy for Teachers primarily support the profession with robust master classes, but they also publish delightful chapbooks in which successful writers offer brief portraits of influential teachers. Get on their mailing list. Get your collection going.

Four Films about Teachers Not Involving Dead Poets

Etre et Avoir (To Be and To Have)
This documentary about a one-room schoolhouse in a small French village is a celebration of patience and teacher compassion—the turtle crawling across the classroom floor in the opening says it all (though the featured teacher later sued the filmmaker for misleading him about the project).

The History Boys
This movie based on Alan Bennett's play of the same name dramatizes two extreme styles of teaching: the charismatic eccentric who creates a vivid student experience on his own terms, and the methodical scholar who prepares students for exam success. An afterschool moment involving a Thomas Hardy poem is worth the entire film.

Monsieur Lazhar
An Algerian immigrant takes over an elementary classroom vacated when a teacher commits suicide. He stumbles to figure out the basics of the job but makes up for his innocence with a tenderness the viewer knows is a product of his own sufferings.

Children Full of Life
A documentary about a remarkable Japanese teacher, who tells his students their goal for the year is to learn how to be happy, leads them to build a community filled with empathy, and models for them what it means to be filled with life.

Two YouTube Clips for Good Measure

Taylor Mali
"What Teachers Make"

Mali is a slam poet with classroom cred, and this three-minute smack down (which led to a book by the same name) is like a primal scream on behalf of under-respected teachers everywhere. I say smack down because he vents and bristles, but Mali is moving too and in a few moments at the mic captures everything I'm defending about the teaching life in these pages: "You want to know what I make?" he says, the challenge and contempt in his voice paving the way for the generosity to come. "I make parents tremble in fear when I call home at around dinnertime. Hi, I'm Mr. Mali, I hope I haven't called at a bad time. I just wanted to talk to you about something your son did today. He said, leave the kid alone; I still cry sometimes, don't you? And it was the noblest act of courage that I have ever seen. I make parents see their children for who they are and who they can be…"

Benjamin Zander
"The Transformative Power of Classical Music"

In this exuberant TED talk, Ben Zander commits to convincing anybody who will lend him five minutes to love classical music. After a moving, guided rendition of a piece by Chopin, his reflections on what it means to be a conductor sound like urgent scripts for every classroom teacher everywhere. "The conductor of an orchestra," he offers, "doesn't make a sound." Instead, he "depends for his power on his ability to make other people powerful." And in a line I still like to share with colleagues whenever I can, he says you can tell you're being an effective conductor because you can see it in your audience's eyes, and when you're not, you don't blame your audience, and you don't even beat yourself up, but still you look inward and ask: "Who am *I* being that my players' eyes are not shining?" A noble, generous high road to stay on with our students.

ACKNOWLEDGMENTS

Gratitude for a book like this should begin and end with teachers. I'd like to thank my colleagues across two and half decades now for caring for me, abiding with me, and making me better. Special thanks to colleagues from my formative years in North Carolina: Carole Hamilton, David Snively, Anthony Risko, German Urioste, Lydia Kim, Vince Janney, Sara Mizelle, Bill Velto, and the entire sterling faculty at Cary Academy. The teacher I became was because of them, and as this book has, I hope, made clear, those years are happily alive inside me. Thanks also to my incomparable colleagues at Avenues The World School in New York City, whose imagination and daring remains, for me, a spur to keep growing and to imagining new things. To Mike Maccarone, Jordan Kravitz, Mike Levy, Sharan Gill, Erin Sheehan, Elie Deu, Kate Howard, Maggie Wollner, Eduardo Guzmán, Tiffany Reedy, Cem Inaltong, Yongling Lu, Mark Gutkowski, Ryan Martin, Matt Scott, and so many others who worked with me side by side to do really difficult things, and who, in the process, modeled fearlessness, grace, humor—and occasional genius.

Because every teacher needs his own team of teachers, heartfelt thanks to my mentors across the years: Tom Bonnell, Skip Mattoon, Ty Tingley, Andy Williams, Michael McElreath, Lorri Hamilton Durbin, and Mary Ehrenworth. I've absorbed their wisdom, but I've valued their joy even more. Special thanks to Will Lidwell and Jeff Clark for almost a decade of support now, and for their tireless belief in me. Working with Jeff and Will has been my own private doctoral program. I hope to never graduate. Thank you to Kate Garrick for reading early versions of this book and making so many shrewd suggestions and for insisting it had life, and thank you to Carlene Bauer for saying, write *this* book, in the first place.

Finally, and with some melancholy, I want to thank and acknowledge the teacher who changed my life: Annette Acuff, who passed away before I could finish this book and hand it to her like an offering. I have tried to pay her tribute in these pages, but I'll offer one more time my lifelong thanks for the quiet waking work she did, which felt like life itself opening—or maybe erupting—inside my younger, vulnerable self. Without a word, she said, behold. I did.

ABOUT THE AUTHOR

Todd Shy has taught for more than twenty-five years in North Carolina, California, and New York. Currently, he is Head of Upper Division at Avenues The World School in New York City.

www.ingramcontent.com/pod-product-compliance
Lightning Source LLC
LaVergne TN
LVHW052021080426
835513LV00018B/2107